WHO ELSE COULD IT BE BUT GOD?

WHO ELSE COULD IT BE BUT GOD?

*My Relationships
Led Me to Him*

CLAYTON REID JONES

TATE PUBLISHING
AND **ENTERPRISES**, LLC

Published by Tate Publishing & Enterprises, LLC
127 E. Trade Center Terrace | Mustang, Oklahoma 73064 USA
1.888.361.9473 | www.tatepublishing.com

Tate Publishing is committed to excellence in the publishing industry. The company reflects the philosophy established by the founders, based on Psalm 68:11,
"The Lord gave the word and great was the company of those who published it."

Book design copyright © 2014 by Tate Publishing, LLC. All rights reserved.
Cover design by Rodrigo Adolfo
Interior design by Jake Muelle
Photography done by Tanja George from Ultimate Media.

Published in the United States of America

ISBN: 978-1-62854-443-5
1. Biography & Autobiography / Personal Memoirs
2. Biography & Autobiography / General
13.11.21

ACKNOWLEDGEMENT

T he ingredients:
First and foremost, the Creator; my lineage—the path in which I was able to get here; my grandparents, Clarence Sterrett and Juanita Sterrett; Dennis Neighbors, Paul Edward Jones, and Evelyn Jones; my parents, Juanita Clarice Gross, Charles Clayton Jones, and Alvin Bernard Gross; my brother, Raymond Norris, and his beautiful family; my sister, Denise Hammond, and her beautiful family; my cousin, Jerry Norris, and all my brothers and sisters by way of my father; all my beautiful aunts, uncles, nieces, nephews, and cousins on both sides of my family; my Wilson Park family whom I consider a part of the foundation I have; my families at Calhoun Street, Cumberland and Carey, Westwood and Mount, thanks for the love.

To every friend I've encountered along the way, you know who you are. Just know that everything you did was needed for me to become the man I am today. God knew what He was doing when our paths crossed.

Special thanks as well to the following who contributed to the project in their own special way: Janet Terrell Jones; Keith Major; my dog for life, Leroy Church; Manny Sterrett; Deneen Edmonds; Juanita Clay; Henry Kennedy;

Rone' Hardworker Thextraordinary; Rakeah Glass (I'll never forget you.); my brother Rodney Greene; Natima Nicole (Team Tima); Sarita McBride; Cerita Powell; Tarris Edlow; Linda McCray; Nikita Chase.

And, of course, I would also like to thank Ms. Bernadette for all that you've done for your grandson over the years. And to my son's parents for doing a great job in raising him. Imperfections are part of the process.

Special thanks to my dear cousin, Jody Lawson, whose courage I dearly love.

To the beautiful Wanda Eaton, for every hour of labor you dedicated to this project and our friendship, I love you and you'll always be my *bestie*.

I like to thank my uncle Earnest and his beautiful wife, Kathy, for their willingness to help me at a crucial time during this process.

To Karuna Maharjan, thank you for sharing your beautiful smile and encouraging words. Just when I wanted to turn back your words were very comforting. We never know how what we say may impact another person, so thank you for allowing your heart to be your guide.

Special thanks to Tanja George and Ultimate Media for adding some visuals to help bring the audience closer to me. You have an incredible eye and please don't stop telling stories.

To my nephew, Miles Norris, family will always be your toughest critics. When I didn't have the courage to share and was needing all the encouragement I could get, I turned to you and you gave me exactly what I needed. Thanks for supporting me in what I wanted to do.

To both the Lane and the Stewart families, you guys are forever in my heart and in my prayers. Thank you so much for being who you are.

Special thanks to my uncle William who now rests. You forced me to confront my truth.

To the woman whom I have made a beautiful daughter with, Ms. Rhonda Brooks, I'd like to thank you also with all my heart.

And last but certainly not the least, to my beautiful children to whom this work is dedicated—Jazmin Monae Jones and Marcus Carter, a.k.a "my sequel"—I love you two and may you forever chase your dreams. With all my heart I'm wishing you all…

Godspeed!

TABLE OF CONTENTS

THE PRELUDE

Being an average black male living in Baltimore City, I've always questioned things. Why was I born in Baltimore City, and why did I live in the neighborhoods I lived? Why couldn't my parents be rich so life could be so much easier? And why was I born black?

It was through a chain of events that I was able to see the truth about life and my existence. From there, something came over me. What came over me, I believe, was God's presence, and I realized I wouldn't change a thing about my life, nor the person that I am; I'm exactly the person that he intended for me to be. It brought me great joy to know who I am and where I come from.

When this project meets completion, let it serve as evidence that God is the source of all things. It's through Him that I'm able to bring you these words. Who else could it be but God?

INTRODUCTION

"Why me?" So many times I've asked myself this question regarding everything in my life. Why am I the person I am? Why were Juanita Clarice Norris (her name at the time) and Charles Clayton Jones my parents? Why was I black? The first time I became aware I was black made me feel like my skin color wasn't the thing to be. Our conditions and the world's depiction of us as being inferior had me feeling this way. It was hard to watch people who looked different from you make all the rules you had to abide by. In addition, these same people seemed to have a tailored life that you could only dream of.

Growing up in the neighborhoods I lived, the "why me?" question plagued me in a different way. Whether you were involved with negative activity or not, you could easily find yourself a victim of some unfortunate circumstances. Processing this realization often had me asking, what if I wasn't so lucky? I used to be scared to death thinking about all the guys growing up whose lives came to an end as teenagers, knowing that at any moment it could've been me.

The early 1980s and all through the 90s were volatile times coming up in Baltimore city. There were so many tragic stories that existed in our neighborhoods, yet despite the despair, we all still managed to experience some love. In its own unique way, the negativity made the love feel even greater, and for a person like me, the love seemed to be what always rescued me in uncertain times. So as I processed this thought, I was able to draw yet another conclusion. The only reason I'm still here and able to experience the life I have is because just like the words that I'm scribing to you now, everything that happens is meant to be.

I wouldn't change one thing about the time I spent living among people with less fortunate circumstances, and along with my family, they remain very much a part of me. Every single thing in life was there to help shape me, and because of the people I grew up with and came to know, I'm exactly who I'm supposed to be. I will never stop carrying the love developed from those times with me inside my heart.

Many people experience major events in their lives, that once they happen, they never look at life the same. Well, for me, it was a series of events that caused my perception to change forever. Never would I have guessed in a million years that something, which started out as a secret that I, along with another, tried to keep from the world, would be the secret that revealed an even greater secret to me. It was all due to a chain of events that shaped what I've come to understand now, to be true.

There I was, a man in his mid-30s, submerged in debt, and feeling like he was facing insurmountable circumstances. It didn't seem like these circumstances would ever go away. Having no solution, my only solution was to run. Running from my circumstances had me change my geographic location, and changing it seemed to have changed everything.

I've never been one to sit and stare at the sky in amazement or marvel at nature. It was, however, in the winter of 2009 when this changed. My new residence's geographic location made the sky, especially the moonlight, provoke a feeling within me. That feeling triggered thoughts that *perhaps we're in a controlled environment, and a light is being shined in on us for observation.* From there, I began thinking maybe my grandmother, who had passed away, was watching over me as I've moved about my life. I've had this thought before, but dismissed it as being just a figment of my imagination. Now as my life develops, I believe this recurring thought remained with me for this moment in time!

For the next month, whenever there was a full moon, it was becoming harder for me to dismiss the thought that *maybe* God and my grandmother were watching over me from afar. While I wasn't completely convinced that God was real, I was always afraid to say he wasn't. Thinking this way would eventually lead me to wonder, what really happens to us when we die?

All my life the thought of death made me very uncomfortable and consumed with fear. Fear that there was nothing left beyond death but eternal darkness. And the way I dealt with this was to convince myself it would be a long time before I would have to face death, so at this time, there was no need to worry. In essence, what I was doing was suppressing my fear of death instead of facing it and trying to overcome it through understanding.

It's funny how a different angle of the same things you've been looking at all your life can change how you see the same things you've been looking at your entire life (humorously). With this change, more change followed, which allowed me to share an experience that's brought the two of us together. To me, these events were extraordinary, and thank you for allowing me to share them through these words. Whenever you notice divine timing with the circumstances regarding your life, I want you all to ask yourselves this simple question: who else could it be but God?

DONNAL

O ver the years, I've created several relationships with people, but one in particular had the most profound impact and ignited a significant change in me. Donnal and I worked together, and from the moment we met, I got a sense I could trust him. Being a person who grew up in a neighborhood where I witnessed a lot of negative behavior create distrust, it was extremely difficult for me to trust anyone. When meeting someone, I would initially keep my guard up until a person proved to be trustworthy. However, I trusted Donnal instantly!

In the beginning, Donnal and I shared very few words, only hello and goodbye. The strangest thing was that through those hellos and goodbyes, I felt a real closeness. I realize now, looking back on those brief exchanges, that no matter how hard you try you can't fake who you really are. Without anyone looking for it, who you are has its own way of presenting itself. Also, the connection two people will share seems to be there from the very start, we just don't realize it until we begin to speak. It's only once we interact that we get a feeling that the relationship was meant to be.

A COMMON INTEREST SHARED

Donnal and I became drawn to one another through our common interests. One in particular was the desire to become rich by gaining material wealth. While Donnal's desire centered on helping others, I wanted to fulfill all of my fantasies and gain the admiration of people. I thought material wealth was the way to do this. This desire was so great that it had me lying about having my own business. I told some people I had a janitorial franchise in addition to my job. The truth of the matter was I did make an attempt to start one, but it never materialized.

Eventually, the false perceptions led a dear friend to recruit me for a legitimate business opportunity. Of course, I immediately jumped at the chance to join the business, are you kidding me, now I would no longer have to lie about being an entrepreneur.

The business was network marketing. Network marketing is commonly referred to as a pyramid business, and its concept is very simple. Once you get started in business for yourself, you help others do the same and at the same time earn percentages from all the business they do. You will also earn percentages from all the people who they will in turn help get started in business. In essence, the more people you get involved in the business from your referrals, the more money you can earn for yourself. My eyes got big just thinking about all the people I knew and believed would jump at this opportunity, especially a business that seemed as simple as this. Donnal was also captivated with the lure of network marketing, and this would be the common thread that would forge our friendship.

The business provides the notion that an average person can achieve above-average success. By no means am I suggesting that either one of us is an average person, or anyone is for that matter, but through our own ignorant perceptions we tend to draw conclusions just by looking at people. When I looked at Donnal for the first time, that very thought came to mind—that he was average. I'm very happy to say that it's through Donnal that I was able to see a true example of an above-average person. His life and passion for wanting more seemed to be driven by his desire to want to help the people in his life. Donnal personified characteristics such as sacrifice, humility, and kindness. He seemed to get great joy in the thought of seeing others succeed and be happy. To me, he was like an angel on earth; someone whose purpose in life was to help God by assisting others.

RECRUITING EACH OTHER FOR BUSINESS

Over the next year or two, I would continue to pursue success in my business, and Donnal and I would find ourselves encouraging one another. Doing this kind of business, your mind gets conditioned to believe the company's products you represent are by far the best in the industry, and nothing else can compare. Although we both understood that neither would take a look at the other's business plan, this never stopped us from trying to convince the other person that their opportunity was the one with the greater potential. Also, the industry's motto implies that you're better off faking it until you make it. As a result, Donnal and I would never share what we already knew, that neither one of us was having any success.

From the attempts to convince one another about business came some very intimate conversations. The conversations moved from the network marketing industry, and I found myself feeling very comfortable opening up to Donnal. He was a person who didn't always need to hear himself speak, but I, on the contrary, was a person who loved to talk. So for me and him to hit it off the way we did seemed to be a natural fit. I shared some of my deepest secrets and truths about my life with him, and he would share some personal things about his. At this point, neither one of us would have to be confronted by the truth that we weren't having much success.

A PERSON WE COULD COUNT ON

As I grew closer to Donnal through our friendship and work relationship, he became a person I would turn to in time of need. The trust was so strong that I found myself comfortable asking Donnal for just about anything, including money. The trust had to be great for me to put my reputation on the line because we all know how people will talk about you when you borrow money.

At that point in my life, my reputation meant everything to me. Without ever saying the words "Man, I won't judge you" verbally, somehow he managed to tell me that with his spirit. Some of the best things you can ever say to a person are sometimes said without words. Every time Donnal would lend me money, I never felt like he was judging me. I also didn't believe he ever talked behind my back about lending me the money. He was the type of person who didn't find pleasure in other people's misfortunes. He found pleasure in the fact that he helped a person in their time of need.

Donnal helped a lot of people that we both worked with, and this made me realize that the special bond he shared with me he also shared with many others. This was not only a testament to his personality, but also a reflection of his character.

Over the years our relationship grew from Donnal being a dependable coworker to someone I considered a brother whom I could rely on. We built this bond without spending a lot of time together outside of work. His ability to ensure my confidence in his loyalty is why I say he showed me what being an above-average person really is. I never met a person quite like him, and I'm not sure that I ever will.

HIS LOYALTY

Two gentlemen Donnal and I worked with introduced Donnal to the network marketing industry. Donnal's bond with and loyalty to these guys would be the reason I couldn't recruit him for business. Donnal could never see himself turning his back on friends, especially friends who presented him with an opportunity that he felt could put his family in a position to become financially secure. His loyalty was what I admired most about him, and it was also what had him holding on to the business too long. I, on the other hand, stopped pursing the business after growing tired of not reaping any rewards.

PERSONAL CHANGES WOULD PUT ME RIGHT BACK IN BUSINESS

The next two years after I stopped pursuing the business, I made some important changes in my life. The biggest change was my living arrangement. I decided to move out of the apartment I was sharing with my daughter and her mom. She and I could no longer see eye-to-eye, so we both felt like we needed a change. With this change, I moved to Cockeysville, Maryland to be closer to my job. After a few months of living there, the strangest thing happened;

I received a business opportunity in the mail. Of all the things I could've received, it was an opportunity to do network marketing.

A representative from a network marketing company dealing with herbal pills sent a videotaped presentation as a means of recruiting individuals. When this happened, I instantly thought about Donnal because this was very similar to what he was marketing. As I sat and watched the presentation, I began feeling confident about the success I could have. My thinking was, "If this person is having success, I know I can too!" I don't like to judge people, but there really wasn't anything extraordinary about this young lady, and she seemed to be having a lot of success.

For the next few weeks, the thought of doing the business again weighed heavily on my mind. Eventually, I gave in to the temptation of giving the business another try. What we were marketing was a service that everyone was using. Our company was positioned in the telecommunications industry. We provided a long-distance service, so I wouldn't have to sell anything to anyone. Why deal with products and inventory when all we did was offer a service you were already paying for? In addition, we supplied the service to the customer at a cheaper rate. This just seemed to make perfect sense. This time I was determined to do the business and have it work for me.

ANOTHER ATTEMPT TO RECRUIT DONNAL

Once I was involved in network marketing again, I immediately spoke to Donnal to see how things were coming along. I have to admit I already knew, so what I was really doing was seeing if he was still willing to remain loyal. My thinking was if I could just get Donnal to understand we were marketing services that everyone had to use, then the chance for his success would be greater.

After speaking with Donnal about this new opportunity, he remained loyal to his business and his friendships. It didn't matter that our relationship had grown so much over that period of time. It also didn't matter that he understood that doing my business provided him with the greater potential. The only thing that mattered to him was his word and the commitment he made to others. Donnal was loyal, and the only thing that could possibly get him to turn away from his loyalty would be a greater loyalty from something very dear to his heart.

MY RELAUNCH WAS A SUCCESS

The successful relaunch of my business was very important because it would play an important role in my relationship with Donnal. In fact, we would eventually get closer as a result of it. The real goal of the business is to become the first person or Independent Representative in an area to expand the concept and company name in that region. This will almost ensure you'll have some level of success. The way to approach it is through word of mouth advertising and recruiting tactics that the network marketing industry has taught you. The object is to launch a meeting in your living room with your closest friends and family, and have that turned into an official hotel briefing, which takes place on a weekly basis. For the first few years, I didn't manage to recruit a single person. Our company had been around for a lot of years, and had several hotel meetings in the area already established. By the time I got involved, I thought the opportunity for growth was limited, and the people who were going to do this kind of business were already doing it.

Deregulation of the entire telecommunication industry would provide the company with a brand new opportunity. Now, instead of doing business solely in the long-distance market, the entire industry would become available to the company. This meant local calling and the most enticing service of them all, the gas and electric service. Everyone who had shelter had to pay for this utility, which gave me the spark I needed to get some momentum going for my business. With this new service, I was able to successfully launch my organization from my living room right into a hotel weekly meeting.

DONNAL JOINS THE BUSINESS

Outside of the new service, recruiting some key individuals at work also helped create some momentum. We had a buzz circulating about the business, which sparked a lot of curiosity. Eventually, that curiosity would lead to more people joining the business. Donnal was now noticing people he had greater loyalty to become part of my organization. He could see the brotherhood forming between us, and to me this was the kind of thing Donnal loved to be a part of. This would have a huge impact on him and would, in fact, eventually influence him to take a look at the business.

After taking a look, Donnal immediately joined the group. He would later share with me he didn't need to see anything. He was going to get involved regardless of the business plan because he didn't want to pass up on the chance to be a part of something so special. He saw four young black males building an organization together. This alone meant more to him than any business opportunity he had ever been a part of. I believe what we were in the process of building was more about a movement and a newfound mindset than it was about money. What we all did in a short period of time was priceless. In a positive way, we were able to influence our coworkers' opinions about young black males. We also did the same thing for some of the people we encountered while doing the business.

SEPARATE WAYS

After a year of doing the business, the momentum died down and eventually came to a stop. The brotherhood that was created remained, but we all went our separate ways. I left the business feeling like I had skills or a gift to do something other than my job, and at the same time feeling like my gift needed to be used in another way. I just didn't know in what way. Despite how I felt about the business, I reluctantly decided to give network marketing one last try, especially after I received a phone call from one of my mentors. It was very necessary for me to make this last attempt because of the profound way it would now have me looking at life.

I realized this business was a mirror image of how the world goes around, and how my compassion wouldn't allow me to take advantage of people for the sake of money. This feeling started resonating strongly in me, and it brought me to the conclusion I had a genuine love and concern for people. There wasn't enough money in this world that could make me take advantage, or justify taking advantage of people's desires to obtain more in life. You see, people can be easily influenced by money, especially when they've never had any. When you withhold the very thing people feel they need to survive, they tend to believe that by obtaining this thing, it will make all their troubles go away. Desperation can set in, leaving people vulnerable and ready to do almost anything to obtain that very thing, which they feel they can't live without. I couldn't profit off of people's desperation. I only had a desire to help them.

Thinking this way, I knew my conscience wouldn't allow me to do the business anymore, and even though the guys continued, it wasn't because they felt they were taking advantage of people. The group of guys I did business with weren't like that, especially Donnal. He was doing the business mainly because of his love for people and desire to help. The difference between me and the guys was simple: No two separate set of eyes will ever see things in exactly the same way. They still continued to see this business as a means to helping others, but I, on the other hand, was beginning to see things in a new light.

OUR BOND

Donnal and I continued to share our special bond, which was even more enriched by our business relationship. Throughout the experience, he constantly showed himself as someone to count on. If not for him, I would have never had the strength to continue for as long as I did. It was why I felt like I was letting him down when I left the business. One thing I love and hold dear to my heart about this point in my life is that he never gave up on me. He would consistently share things about the business with me, especially all the progress being made, if only to get me to rejoin the group. He didn't encourage me because he had something to gain if I rejoined. With me in the business, it could never impact Donnal from a financial standpoint. He was a part of my organization, not the other way around. He encouraged me because of his desire to see us all succeed. This made my love for him grow even stronger.

Donnal's heart and his intent were so pure, and I believe that he was indeed one of the last real good guys. Donnal would wish the best for everyone and lend a helping hand to a friend in need. Oftentimes, he would share stories with me on how he knew people would talk about him behind his back, and yet still help those very same people. He was always there when you needed him. Donnal had this way about him where, in some instances that you found yourself in need and at some point became stressed about it, he would show up and rescue you. Sometimes he wouldn't give you an answer right away, leaving you with the feeling of uncertainty. But right before you would lose hope, there was Donnal to ease your mind. At least, this is what he did for me.

Thinking back, I can't remember a time when Donnal wasn't able to help me when I asked him for money. He always came through for me, never asking for anything in return. No matter how much I expressed how willing I was to help, he would never ask for it. The only way I found out he needed help was through the intimate talks we shared, which would always come out after the help was no longer needed.

Looking back at our relationship, I feel like I may have helped him by giving him an outlet to vent his frustrations. Even though we didn't talk or spend much time together outside of work, I always knew Donnal and I were close like brothers. What I didn't know was how much Donnal talked about me to his family and friends. One day, things began to take a turn for the worse.

GROWING TIRED

Donnal suffered from diabetes throughout his life. I can recall a time when complications from his diabetes would land him in the hospital. I wasn't sure he would pull through, but when he did, it was such a relief for me; more so because I didn't have to entertain thoughts of him dying. I realize this is a certainty for all of us, but I just can't seem to grow comfortable thinking about it, especially when it came to him. I didn't want to think about him ever leaving us. To me, he was too much of a nice guy for us to lose.

The thought of what could've happened, I believe, got to Donnal as well. He talked to me about his plans to lose weight and take better care of himself. From that conversation, I invited him to join me at the track in the mornings when he got off of work. I thought that him having a partner would help keep him motivated and make things a little easier in the beginning. It was the least I could do for someone who had been there for me all the time. Unfortunately, we never got the chance to exercise together. Time went on and what happened was no longer thought about. I felt like he had his disease under control and that maybe it was no longer a threat. He kept saying he wasn't ready yet, and soon things would change forever in both of our lives.

I remember sharing a conversation with Donnal right before our Christmas break. As we talked, I could sense Donnal was growing tired. The burden of always helping others and feeling like other people weren't giving him the same consideration seemed to be taking its toll on him. The conversation we shared was about a good friend of his who was always taking but never giving, or even considering that Donnal may have needed help every once in a while. I believed he felt like he was being taken for granted, and all he really wanted was for his friends to consider him the way he always did them. As he explained his point, I could see for the first time he was frustrated, and as a result, I can never forget the look on his face that day. In his face I saw pain that didn't appear to be physical. No, this pain was emotional, and it appeared that Donnal was crying out for help that no one, not even me, could administer.

The most compelling thing taken from the conversation was the feeling I got from looking at him. I felt like I couldn't help, and that had me not wanting to fall short when it came to helping people that were closest to me ever again. Seeing him in this way made me feel very inadequate as a friend. In the days that followed, it was confirmed that Donnal, in fact, was growing tired. He was in a lot of pain.

DONNAL HOSPITALIZED

On December 27, 2009, I received a phone call from my cousin, Leroy telling me that Donnal suffered a stroke on Christmas night and that he was rushed to the hospital. He saw the news posted by a friend and fellow coworker, Terri Birchfield, on the social network they both were a part of. When I heard the news, I was stunned. Even though I knew about his health problems, I wasn't ready to hear this. I thought his condition was under control.

For the next few days, the feeling that I had an obligation to go see Donnal in the hospital plagued my mind. I thought what kind of friend would I be if I didn't go? Especially when all he did for me was to be there whenever I needed him? It was such a struggle for me. Whenever the time came for me to make a sacrifice for others, it always seemed like it was too much to bear. At times I was so lazy, but I knew I had to get over myself and make this sacrifice. This was something I had to do; I wouldn't forgive myself if I didn't.

Like all things that didn't involve me getting some sort of instant gratification, for days I had put off my plans of seeing Donnal using work as the excuse. When I got my first day off for the holiday, I continued to procrastinate, saying I would just go tomorrow. Tomorrow came and the next day was New Year's, and I knew this would probably create another excuse. With that in mind, I was beginning to feel a sense of urgency about going.

Word got back to me that Donnal's sisters were asking about me, they wanted to know if I was coming to see him. Having his sisters inquire about me really brought confirmation to the friendship I believed we shared. At this point, I had met only his sister Zelda on one occasion, and spoke briefly to his sister Belinda over the phone regarding business. That same morning, I also received a phone call from my friend Keith. Keith wanted to know if he could ride with me to see Donnal. These two things made me feel like I had to go. The last thing I wanted was for Keith and Donnal's sisters to feel like I didn't care.

Once Keith and I arrived at the hospital, I was afraid. Fear was building up inside of me as we made our way to Donnal's room. I was so afraid of death that it made it very difficult for me to visit people in the hospital, especially when death was such a strong possibility in their circumstances. When I arrived at his room, the fear had me making excuses for not wanting to go in. My excuse was that I couldn't stand to see Donnal this way, which was partially true. But the real reason was, thinking about death made me revisit my thought that when we die, there's nothing left for us but eternal darkness. Being totally consumed with fear, a very close friend of Donnal's relieved me of it. With a few simple words, he was able to bring a sense of peace about the whole thing. He simply said, "Go in there and spend some time with your man." And just like that, I became at ease. It made me feel like Donnal was waiting for me to come.

Before I got to the hospital, I had a preconceived notion of what Donnal would look like. Because of my fear, I pictured the most horrific image imaginable. When I got close to Donnal to take a good look, he didn't look bad at all. In fact, he looked just like he did the last time I was with him. The only difference was that he had a tube coming out of the top of his head, and his eyes were closed, and pain was no longer a part of his expression. With this, I was beginning to become more at ease while standing over him. They told me he was aware of our voices, and I can remember standing there, just staring at him and wondering if he knew I was there. The more I stared, the easier things became, and eventually I became comfortable enough to talk. I told Donnal I wanted him to pull through and that I would be there for him when he needed me. I also found words to say to his family, especially his sister Zelda. I began to share how I felt toward him and how he was always there for me. I can remember shedding some tears while I was trying to hold them back, and at the same time telling his sisters "Donnal had a lot of my secrets lying there with him in that bed." We all smiled and shook our heads in agreement because it made sense to all of us, knowing the type of person he was.

My visit came to an end, and at that time I was extremely comfortable. I was looking forward to coming back the next day because I had a feeling that he was going to pull through after all. I felt for sure that all he needed was for his friends to be there, the same way he was there for us in the past. As I was leaving, I mentioned to Zelda and Belinda I would be returning the next day. I really believed my presence was felt by Donnal, and it was going to be my presence that would help bring him out of his coma. Maybe it was my vanity that had me thinking this way, but nevertheless I was over my fear and ready to be there for Donnal like he had always been there for me in the past.

Later that day while I was in the supermarket, I received a phone call from Belinda. She was very cautious as she explained to me I wouldn't be able to go see Donnal the next day. The doctors suggested to the family that visitation be limited because Donnal seemed to become agitated. Belinda didn't want me to feel as if I was the problem, so she was very careful in saying that it wasn't me being there, and she knew Donnal loved the fact that I was there. It was the doctors who felt it was best to try and keep him as calm as possible in his current state.

After she explained things to me, I didn't get upset at all. My thinking was that Donnal was responding to me because of her opening statement. She said, "Clayton, as soon as you left something happened, it's normal but he became agitated. The doctors said that sometimes too many visitors can make the patient become uneasy." See, the key thing Belinda said was that after I left, something happened. I'm a person that struggles with vanity, and, for me, that meant I was making a difference. I felt Donnal was reacting to me leaving, and as long as I was there, he was calm. I got excited, I felt the agitation was a sign that Donnal was coming out of his coma, so I called Keith to tell him the news.

I shared the news with Keith that we couldn't go back the next day, and that I also felt Donnal was responding to us being there. Having suggested this, I realize now how much of a problem my vanity really is. Donnal had the people he was closest to and cared the most about by his bedside. If anyone was going to have that much of an impact, it would be his family and not me. Realizing this now, I felt that it was important for me, after all, to feel this way. I needed to think this way in order for me to come to the realization that it wasn't by chance that Donnal's life would have such a profound impact on me.

DIDN'T SEE IT COMING

It was Sunday, January 3, 2010. I was watching the Ravens play the Raiders when my phone rang. I looked down to see who was calling and the caller ID read Donnal Lane. If I try to describe to you my excitement I wouldn't do it any justice. In my heart, I truly believed Donnal was going to pull through, so when I received that phone call, I jumped up with excitement and said, "This is Donnal on the phone! I knew he would pull through!" When I answered the phone,

I heard a voice on the other end say, "Hello." I almost said Donnal's name, but for some reason, I didn't. I think it was because I didn't want to be impolite, so I let that person speak. Then the person on the other end of the phone said to me in a very short statement, "Yo, Clayton, Donnal passed away." The minute I heard this, I lost all feeling. I couldn't believe what I was hearing. I realized then it was Donnal's nephew, Terrance, calling using Donnal's phone. This news was so hard for me to believe because my heart was set on Donnal pulling through.

After that phone call, the football game no longer had relevance. All I could think about was how I couldn't believe Donnal was gone. I had family members pass away, and no death other than my cousin Curtis's had this much of an impact on me. I believe it was the timing that made this grab my attention. Donnal and I were close, but it wasn't like he and I grew up as childhood friends. We both had people in our lives that we shared greater bonds with, but because of the bond we shared, I developed a strong desire to want to help his family.

HOW COULD I HELP?

Finding a way to help Donnal's family would dominate my thoughts. Donnal had always given me money in the past, and now I felt his family could use some. The problem was I had none to give, so in what other way could I help? I became consumed with this thought because I wanted so desperately for his family to see how much he really meant to me. After giving it a lot of thought, I couldn't seem to come up with anything. For the next four days, I was carrying around the burden of wanting to help the family of a man who gave to me all the time when he really didn't have it to give. Of course, I put money in a card that was being passed around for co-workers to sign, but that wasn't enough for me based on our relationship.

As the days went on, I kept this to myself for fear that people would become aware of the fact I was struggling to contribute. I certainly wouldn't communicate these thoughts to his sisters. I knew they would just tell me the thought of wanting to help was enough. Without ever expressing the truth to anyone, I received a phone call on January 7, 2010; Donnal's sister Belinda had a question. The family wanted to know if I would consider being a pallbearer for Donnal during his Homegoing Service. It didn't register at first, but when it finally sank in I couldn't believe what I was hearing.

Donnal had so many friends he shared a closer bond with, so I never gave being a pallbearer any thought. The family decided to have two sets, one to carry Donnal from the church to the hearse, and the other to carry him from the hearse to the burial site. I thought this was perfect. Now I had a personalized way to help his family. I was gleaming with joy because of the peace that was given to me in that moment. What I said to Belinda after it all registered in my mind was, "It would be my honor to carry Donnal." After the phone call, I felt relief beyond measure. Now the question became: How did they know I needed help with helping them? This was such a coincidence, the family provided me with exactly what I needed, and at the precise time it was needed. All I could say was "Wow."

THE SPIRIT LIVES ON

The next day was Donnal's viewing. I was at work and wouldn't be able to make it, but that was just fine with me because now I had a role to play during the Homegoing Service. As my shift was nearing its end, I received yet another phone call from Belinda. Belinda had another question, and this time, she and the family wanted to know if I would be willing to say a few words on Donnal's behalf. I was shocked. I never saw this coming. While Belinda was talking over the phone, I was also becoming more and more nervous. I thought that if I were already this nervous over the phone, then how much more when the time came for me to share a few words during the service?

Belinda and the rest of the family remembered I spoke in front of people when I did the business and they thought this would be easy for me. They never shared the meeting place in Baltimore, so they were unaware of how I would break out into a nervous sweat during the presentations. My first response was no. I didn't really feel comfortable doing this. First off, I didn't want to mess things up. Secondly, I didn't feel I was the right person for the job. The last thing I wanted was for me to start sweating and have that shift the focus off Donnal and the words I would share.

Another thing that I found very interesting was the fact that Donnal was trying to get me back in business before he left. He felt like we all should come back together again sharing the spotlight. When we did the business together, it was a group of us that built a great story. My best friend at the time was my partner in business, and we conducted the presentations together. We had another friend who was very close to Donnal in our organization that also shared the spotlight. I mentioned Donnal had greater loyalty to some other people in his life, and his good friend who shared the spotlight with us was one of those people. I also found out later that this friend was the reason Donnal got into business with us in the first place.

With regard to what the family was asking of me, I couldn't turn down the request. Deep down it was something I really wanted to do anyway, and my thinking was, "This is the least I could do." All that was required of me was to say a few words on his behalf and not go over three minutes. Belinda also made me feel at ease because when I told her I wasn't sure what I would say, she told me to say exactly what I said to the family in the hospital. She told me she thought those words were perfect. When Belinda and I ended our phone conversation, things began to shift with my understanding. I also like to mark that time as the time when things began to happen. After hanging up the phone, I sat for a few minutes, evaluating what just took place, and suddenly I experienced one of the greatest joys I've ever had the pleasure of experiencing. In that very instance, as clear as you are reading these words, I could see and feel Donnal laughing at me. That's right, he was laughing! And he wasn't just laughing, he was elated! I knew for certain this could only be him.

As I mentioned before, Donnal was the type of person who would help you out of a jam, and sometimes he wouldn't give you an answer right away. After things became a burden for you, and when you least expected, he would deliver you from your stress, and would laugh with you when he did. This is exactly what I felt he was doing for me at the time. I strongly felt that it could only be him. His family had no way of knowing I was carrying the burden of wanting to help them, and I certainly don't believe in this much of a coincidence. As a matter of fact, I don't believe in coincidences anymore.

In his own way, Donnal was going to get me speaking in front of people again. He used to enjoy it when I did, and he also believed it was one of my gifts. Without question, I knew this was his doing. In light of all the things taking place inside of me, I knew now for the first time in my life that when we pass on, it's not the end for us; the spirit really does live on. After his death, Donnal was still doing things he did when he was alive, and that included helping me out of a jam. It's not by chance that when I had this realization, the first words out of my mouth were, "We don't die! Oh my God, we don't die!" I believe these events took place so

I would utter those words and experience this new found realization. At this point in my life, this was so significant because this was my greatest fear. Like I said, I was afraid there was nothing left for us but eternal darkness. Not only would the realization ease my mind when it came to this fear, but it would also influence the things I thought about in the days to come. If not for me changing my geographic location, which allowed me to see the moon the way I did, these thoughts may not have been in the forefront of my mind.

Donnal had now given me something more than money could ever give for the moment; he gave me hope when it came to my fear of death. Of course I wasn't completely over it, but it was through him I was put on a path that would lead me to a greater understanding. When I felt Donnal's presence that day and saw him laughing at me, this was something I had to share. I was so overjoyed with the way I felt that every time I tried to explain what happened, it brought tears to my eyes.

I did manage to share my story with a close friend who was on her way to view Donnal's body. She said she could believe what I was saying, and that it didn't seem far-fetched at all. She was a person that strongly believed the body will perish but the spirit lives on. It wasn't by chance that I was able to get the story out to her when I couldn't seem to do it with others. She supported me in my belief, which brought me more confirmation. Out of all the people I could've shared this with, I found someone who, instead of creating doubt in my mind, helped keep me focused on what I now believe to be true.

While I was sitting at my desk thinking about what I was going to say at the service, I tried to come up with things heartfelt that my other coworkers would agree upon. Then suddenly, I received a phone call from the coworker I shared my story with. She was at the funeral home viewing the body. When I answered the phone, she said to me, "Clayton! You are not going to believe what your boy is doing right now." "What boy?" I said. She said, "Donnal." And I was, like, "Huh?" Then she said, "Yeah, Donnal. Take a guess on what you think he is doing right now?" I couldn't because I was at a loss for words, so she said, "You're not gonna believe this, but your boy, Donnal, is smiling right now." She reiterated, "It looks like Donnal has a smile on his face right now." All I could say was, "Are you serious?" She said, "Yes, he has a smile on his face right now!" The words that came from my mouth in that instance were, of course, "Oh my God." After that, I couldn't hold back the tears.

Now can you imagine how I was feeling? The very thing I felt so strongly about had just been confirmed with physical evidence. If I was overjoyed before, this had to be total bliss. Tears came to my eyes, and no one could suggest to me that the spirit doesn't live on. No one could suggest to me that even through his death, Donnal wasn't still doing the things that he did for me when he was alive. See, now I had my proof, Donnal decided to give me a sign it was him. The sign was his smile. He made sure a close friend would see this, hours later after I bared witness to it through his spirit. And not just any friend, but the friend he knew would call me on the phone to tell me what she just saw. It was like he was there when I shared the story, and as I think about it, he had to be.

I would receive even more confirmation the next day during the service. I got a surprise when the time arrived for me to speak. When my name got called, I was greeted by my best friend and Donnal's close friend. The family had arranged for all of us to speak one after another, sharing stories about Donnal. What a surprise! I knew this too had to be him. This was exactly what Donnal wanted and had recently discussed. For me, it felt like old times minus the sweating and remembering this still makes me smile. For some reason, I never got nervous when the time arrived for me to speak, and now I realize why. I didn't get nervous because the words I shared came straight from my heart. I believe this was the difference from when I spoke in front of people while doing the business. The words that I shared then didn't have my conviction along with them. My body was reacting to my disbelief in what I was saying. This proved to be an incredible turning point for my life. Not only was this a strong confirmation, but it would also be a focal point for me in the days to come.

Now my mind was prepared for an even greater revelation, but at the time I had no idea what was being done. This revelation would not only change the way I viewed death, but it would also alter the way I lived my life from this point on. Nothing about life would ever look the same again, and with this, I would like for Donnal's family to know that by no means did Donnal's death come in vain. I believe Donnal served a great purpose from his lot in life, and he served an even greater purpose for me. Donnal's life and death served the purpose of conditioning my mind to understand the events to come. Things that would unfold had me paralyzed in my thinking that all I was be able to do was talk about my recent experience with Donnal and about my newfound belief that the spirit lives on. This thinking was so important because it enabled me to understand the next thing to be revealed. Also, it forced me to never forget my friend and brother, Morris Donnal Lane, as my life moves forward. How can I ever forget the man who, through his spirit, helped me face my biggest fear—death—and he also helped me understand that through great loss comes great gain. I don't believe I will ever be completely over my fear of death—although I try to never say never—but for that period of time, I was able to experience great comfort when thinking about it.

One of the greatest things you can ever do for a person is to relieve them of their fear, even if it's just momentarily. Donnal Lane's passing signified a new awakening in me, and if not for this awakening the greatest revelation of them all wouldn't have been understood once it was revealed. Even though I had become paralyzed in my thinking, and it all revolved around the spirit living on, I still didn't expect the events that were to follow. In the days that followed, I was able to gain a great understanding, and I would like to thank my friend and brother, Morris Donnal Lane. I want you to know you'll always be remembered and loved, by yours truly. May you rest in peace.

RONALD

After I said goodbye to Donnal, I spent my days wondering about the impact I might have on people when I pass away. This had me examine my treatment of others, and in the process, I developed a desire to be the best person I could be. As a result of pride, I overlooked one of the most important relationships I've ever had in my life. The relationship was between me and one of my best friends, Ronald Stewart.

Our relationship had been damaged because of trivial matters, and what better time was there than the present to repair a relationship that has existed for over thirty years. Ronald and I first met as foes on the little league baseball field at age nine. After baseball, we didn't get reacquainted until high school, and our relationship didn't become close until we attended the same trade school after we graduated.

For two years in trade school, we found ourselves around each other every morning, noon, and night. I needed money to help pay for school, so Ronald helped me land a part-time job in the evenings where he worked. We also shared common interest, so our social lives were linked as well. This had me spending just as much time with Ronald as I was spending with myself. For two people, you really couldn't get any closer.

With all the time being spent together, it was only natural we got on each other's nerves. Just like all best friends do, Ronald and I would bicker with each other over every little thing. And just like all best friends do, we would go periods of time not speaking to one another. The silence wouldn't last very long because Ronald would do something or say something funny to make me laugh. I felt this was his way of saying "I'm sorry", or his way of getting things back to normal.

I believe the awkwardness of us spending time with each other without speaking got to us more than any other problems we faced. Now, looking at our relationship thirty years later, I believe neither one of us really wanted to spend our lives without having the other person in it, but pride wouldn't allow two grown men to express this to one another. Eventually, this would become the reality for me.

DISTANCE

As I stated earlier, I overlooked several opportunities to be a better friend to Ronald. Ronald decided to take an important step in his life; he was getting married. With that, he asked me to be the best man. I felt extremely honored by his request since he had friends in his life that were there since his childhood, and he and I didn't become as close as we were until trade school. This really confirmed to me how he felt, so I couldn't let him down. I accepted his offer, but when the time came for me to stand up for Ronald, I wasn't there. Not only did I not show up, I told him a lie as my excuse for not showing up. To add insult to injury, I didn't give him advanced notice. I put it off until the last minute, leaving him the challenge of making other arrangements with little time. How selfish was that? Being so self-centered, I never once stopped to think about how this might affect him and our relationship. When I said I never stopped to think about it, I literally never gave it any thought. I was too busy thinking about myself.

Ronald became very disappointed in me and became absent from my life for years. The sad thing about it was I didn't even notice. How do you manage to not notice your best friend missing from your life for a few days, let alone for a few years? Being so consumed with myself was making it hard for me, to look at anything other than me. So to answer my own question, that was how.

To make matters worse, he and I would eventually live within walking distance from one another in Cockeysville. He managed to stay away, and I did very little to reach out. This dynamic wasn't dawning on me until one day when we had a snowstorm. Being bored and stuck indoors, I guessed we both were looking for something to do. This made He and I reach out to one another, and he and his wife decided to come down to my apartment and play cards. While waiting for their arrival, I had a very peculiar thought. I said to myself, "Damn, it's been a long time since I've seen Ronald. I wonder why." Honestly speaking, I had forgotten all about being a no-show on the day of his wedding.

Ronald and his wife made it down, we played cards, and everything seemed to be just fine. Ronald never mentioned a word about the wedding, and I remained completely unaware of any problem. We both enjoyed each other's company, like we never spent any time apart. We laughed, we ate, we drank, all in all we had a great time. In my mind, I felt we re-established our connection and were now ready to resume our friendship. Unfortunately, that wasn't the case, and shortly after, I realized Ronald was once again absent from my life, and for the life of me, I couldn't figure out why.

Ronald worked for a company I previously worked for. Through my family members who worked there, I was able to help him land a job, and this made it easy for me to stay abreast of some of the changes that were going on in his life. Some years had passed, and word got back to me that he and his wife were having trouble, which would eventually lead to them splitting up. After the breakup, I discovered he was dating my cousin, Jody. Their relationship had grown, so they decided to buy a house together. After getting settled into the house, they had a party we all were invited to. I got excited about going because I hadn't seen him since the snowstorm, and I believed this would be a great opportunity for us to rekindle the friendship. I remember feeling extremely happy for the two of them. We spent most of the day laughing and joking, but I also got a sense there was still some tension between us. When I tried to open up, he was cold, and I just couldn't put my finger on the reason.

After seeing and feeling the cold reaction, it didn't surprise me when things went back to the way they were. Instead of me overlooking or dismissing the fact something was wrong, now I found myself pondering the thought more often. I had no choice but to think about our relationship because now Ronald's name was being mentioned in family conversations.

As a result of my going back to one of my old barbers, I began seeing Ronald in the barbershop on a weekly basis, which would conveniently lead to us having conversations. Eventually, what came out of those conversations was a need for him to confide in me. Ronald and Jody were experiencing some problems they both felt were irreconcilable, and the day he came to explain his side of things was the day we started forming another bond. This would also mark the start of me gaining clarity about the problem that plagued our relationship.

THE CONVERSATION

W hile leaving the barbershop, Ronald asked if I had a few minutes to talk. I had no idea what this was about, but I felt good that he wanted to do this in a private setting because to me this felt like progress. We decided to talk in the car. We began with general conversation and a few laughs before he eventually opened up. Like most of us do when confessing a wrong we've done to someone, we look for empathy; we start by telling all the wrong things that were done to us. It's the way we try to justify our behavior.

Ronald said to me, "I feel like Jody is taking advantage of me. I'm not getting what I deserve from her. When I come home from work, all I want is some affection and she refuses to give me any. When I reach out to her and show signs of affection, there's always an excuse. Clayton, we don't even sleep in the same bed anymore." He went on to say how he tried to provide anything she wanted financially and that alone should warrant her fulfilling his needs. Ronald told me he felt very unappreciated and disrespected at times. He gave me the feeling like he couldn't take much more.

One day, everything reached its apex with them two. Jody said some things to Ronald during an argument, which made him feel belittled. Not to make any excuses for his behavior, but I also understood nothing will push a man's buttons like when a woman deliberately disrespects him. Ronald said, "In that moment, I felt like she was testing my manhood. I lost all my control and I pushed Jody down on the bed. Clayton, I didn't hit her, but I never should've put my hands on her." Then he looked me right in my eyes as a man does when he owns up to his mistakes and said, "While I held her down on the bed, I spit in her face." "You did what?" I replied. He said, "I spit on her."

I couldn't believe what I was hearing. Never in my life would I have imagined Ronald doing something so disrespectful and despicable. I just didn't think he had it in him. Ronald was always a gentleman with the ladies based on what I've come to know about him. He was always pampering his girlfriends trying to make them happy with him because of his insecurities. I don't believe he felt like he was very desirable to women so in exchange, he would do a lot of things for them trying to win their affection. I've witnessed girlfriends from his past doing things that seemed as if they had little regard for his feelings, but he never reacted this way. So for him to do this to Jody made me very disappointed, but that was nothing compared to the disappointment he was feeling toward himself.

Ronald decided to tell me what happened before I heard it through family chatter. Maybe he was thinking he needed to do some damage control for fear the news would end our relationship altogether. Based on the way

I felt toward him, I tried not to ever pass judgment, and I never let his relationship with Jody come between us and vice versa. Jody was my cousin and like a sister to me, I love her dearly, but there are some things you just can't interfere with. Now, I would never stand by and allow someone to put their hands on her, regardless of the circumstances, although at the same time I would never get involved with her household or domestic affairs. I would just be there for her if she needed me. I also felt the same way toward Ronald. If not for Ronald feeling uncertain about how I would react to what he did, we never would've had that talk in the car. That talk and my reaction led to us spending more time together and embracing each other sincerely. I believe the way I reacted to the situation made Ronald feel like I could understand. I also believe he realized that despite all the things I've done in the past, I was his friend, and maybe it was time for him to offer me a little bit of forgiveness as well.

I FINALLY UNDERSTOOD

A t this point, I was still in the dark about why Ronald had been so distant. Over the years, he held onto the disappointment of me not being there for the wedding. As I mentioned before, Ronald had friendships with others much longer than the friendship we shared. For him to ask me to be the best man should've made me realize what it meant for him to have me standing by his side. It's only now that I realize how much Ronald loved having me as his friend. He loved hanging out with me because he liked my style. Sometimes we gravitate toward people we feel garner a certain level of respect. We like to associate ourselves with people we think are cool, and that others share that same admiration for. What he didn't realize was I wasn't all that I cracked myself up to be. The real reason I backed out of my obligation was because, in my opinion, I couldn't afford to be the best man. Since I had an image I was trying to uphold, I didn't have the courage to let him know I was broke. As the Best Man, it was my responsibility to have a Bachelor's Party. I could barely pay my rent, car note, and keep food on the table, let alone pay for a party for him. Inside my heart, I would've loved to have the party, but the reality was I just couldn't afford it.

There was also the issue of supplying the girls, and with this, I would run the risk of yet another one of my secrets being exposed. I wasn't the ladies' man people thought I was. I was very happy and content being in my relationship with Rhonda and going home to her and my baby girl every night. She and I had just moved into our first apartment, and although we were struggling at the time, we were happy. So instead of me confiding in Ronald and telling him the truth, I decided to lie and make an excuse, which damaged our relationship. All this time, he had been holding this in without telling me, and it had hurt him to his heart. I guess the same foolish pride that didn't allow me to come clean with my issues had him in a choke hold as well.

Feeling the emptiness of ending the relationship with my cousin, Ronald decided to gravitate back to me. He needed comfort and support and realized I would always be there for him despite some of my actions from the past. He also realized in order for him to offer me forgiveness, I would first need to be made aware of what was troubling him. So with us spending more time together, he finally relinquished the problem on his heart after all those years.

Hanging out at my apartment one day, he decided to tell me all the bitterness and distance between us, stemmed from me not being there at his wedding. Finally, it all made sense, and I wondered why this didn't dawn on me before. Nevertheless, this was now giving me the opportunity to see myself for who I really was. Everything became so clear to me. I was selfish, and now moving forward, all I wanted was to be honest with Ronald about everything.

From this point on, I felt we shouldn't let any problems fester between us, and if anything would be wrong, we should express it to the other person and move on. This also inspired me to share with him my real reason for not participating in the wedding. Like a real friend, he understood and expressed a desire to not let anything like that come between us again. Nothing from the past would matter anymore because now I had my friend back in my life, just like it used to be. This was exactly what we both needed, so this couldn't have happened at a better time.

HIS NEW RELATIONSHIP

All of what transpired between Ronald and me happened over a ten-year period. I had experienced some personal growth and was living alone completely single, so this left me with a lot of time on my hands. In other words, I was beginning to experience loneliness. Ronald, with what he just went through with my cousin, was probably feeling the same. This made the conditions great for him and me to restore our friendship. It started with us spending every weekend together and learning that we both like shooting pool. This led to us spending countless hours at the pool hall. It went from going on Saturdays for a few hours to us spending all day Saturday and then going back on Sunday. From there, we hung out at my apartment, and with Ronald there most of the time, my neighbors also got the chance to get to know him. We hung out, cooked on the grill, drank, and this became our regular routine. Life was good, we both were supplying the other one with the companionship we both needed.

Even with all the growth I had experienced, I was still shallow when it came to my image. I wasn't ready to confide all my truths to him, and later this would cost me our friendship yet again. Thinking about this now has made little sense. Ronald was my man, and I felt so at ease with him as opposed to some of my other friends, so confiding my truths should've been easy, especially because when I hung out with him I could be myself without putting on any airs. The reason I couldn't admit everything was because I still enjoyed the way Ronald looked at me, or at least the way I thought he looked at me, like I was a lady's man. Trying to keep this image, I never let on to the fact I was lonely. To keep the perception going, I was able to muster up a few relationships cosigning the fact, but the reality was I was hoping one of those relationships turned out to be the one I was looking for.

Ronald met two different young ladies whom I shared a fondness for, and I would just act as if they were one of many. Even though I kept this charade going, I can't honestly say Ronald believed me. He was spending enough time around me to know better, so the only person I was probably fooling was myself. I just think Ronald didn't care much. He had the type of sense of humor that would have him being amused by the whole thing. But nevertheless, it felt so good having him back in my life like old times, and none of the other things really mattered.

Ronald and I had firmly reestablished the friendship. We were helping each other out with money issues, talking on a daily basis, and keeping our weekend routine going. He would come to me with his issues and I would turn to him. I believe we both were so conscious about our past that it made us very determined to not let anything come between us ever again. Whenever Ronald gave me money, I always made sure I gave it back and tried my best to give him money if he needed it. The last thing I wanted was for money to create a problem in our relationship. With us establishing trust when it came to money, Ronald felt confident it would be okay to help me in another way. What he did was offer to let me onto his cell phone account. My credit at the time would not allow me to establish my own, so he, being a good friend, decided to lend me some assistance.

I joined his plan and things seemed to be working out just fine. In the meantime, Ronald found himself in a new relationship with a beautiful young lady, and I couldn't have been happier for him, even though I knew this relationship would start to affect our time together. Whenever Ronald became involved with a woman, she became the center of his world. With the way this young lady looked coupled with her personality, I couldn't say that I blamed him.

As weeks went by, it was just as I expected—our routine on the weekends dwindled away. Ronald would only come spend time with me when his girlfriend was busy, and I was now being used to fill time. This worked out perfectly for me because one of the aforementioned relationships I had experienced was during this time. It was new, so I was spending a lot of my time with her on the weekends. Like all new things, the novelty would wear off and soon my weekends became free again. Ronald would still find time for us to play pool, but the majority of his time was spent with his girlfriend. She had a daughter, and this was the type of relationship Ronald always seemed to find himself in. He didn't have children of his own but always wanted some, so this would have him becoming attached to the kids.

I believe what hurt Ronald the most about his divorce was the relationship he shared with her son. Ronald spent a great deal of time with his stepson and never considered the word "step." But after the marriage ended, the boy could no longer be a part of his life. With his new relationship, I believed the little girl was helping to fill that void. The activities were different, but the way he felt was probably the same. He loved his time with her, and now Ronald was feeling like he had found a home again. Honestly speaking, I was starting to become a little jealous.

PROBLEMS

I became accustomed to my time being cut short with Ronald, but one weekend I noticed him spending an unusual amount of time at my place. I didn't pay it much attention, but when the following weekend came and he did the same thing, I became suspicious. I was noticing a pattern developing; Ronald was spending time with me on the weekends. One weekend, he actually never left. I fell asleep and woke up only to find him still in the chair I left him in when I went to bed. I knew there was a problem, but I also knew how sensitive he was about discussing it, so I decided not to say anything until he was ready to bring it up.

In the past, there were a few issues but nothing too serious. It was about his girlfriend needing a little space. Before it happened, I suggested to Ronald he might want to give her some, and his response showed he was agitated. This made it clear he didn't like hearing that from me. I understand both sides of it. To me, there's nothing wrong with a man devoting so much of his time and attention to a woman, but for some reason they seem to become bored. It's a natural reaction to be tempted by what we don't have, I don't know why, but some women prefer a man who leaves them on edge. It's the old cliché—a woman wants a bad boy. So when I noticed him spending more time with me, the first thought that came to mind was she probably felt smothered. I decided not to say a word because no one likes being around a person who thinks they know it all, even if that person may be speaking the truth.

Determined not to push the issue, I waited until Ronald could no longer ignore the obvious. He knew I realized there was a problem, and you can only carry frustration and hurt around for so long. Eventually, it will start to get the best of you. From there you're left with no choice but to release it. Ronald shared with me that he and his girlfriend seemed to be moving in different directions. He also told me he was back staying with his mother. Knowing Ronald as well as I did, I knew this hurt his feelings, even though he did a good job of not letting it show. If all of your relationships end in the same way, it can start to play on the insecurities you may have about yourself. In my opinion, there was nothing wrong with Ronald. He was a great person that any woman in her right mind would've felt blessed to have. With everything that he was facing, he seemed more on edge, and it wouldn't take much for him to get upset. With us spending more time together, this was exactly what happened. A new problem arose, which, in my opinion, should've never become a problem.

THE FINAL STRAW

With Ronald and I being very open about money matters and helping each other out on occasion, it caught me by surprise to have problems arrive concerning our cell phones. One morning, I tried to use my phone but wasn't able to because the phone had been cut off. I was certain I paid the bill, so I immediately called Ronald. Ronald explained to me it was a third person sharing the bill and due to his tardiness, the service was interrupted. I understood, but this irritated me mainly because of my ego. I didn't want people to have the perception I couldn't pay my bill, even though this was the reality sometimes. If it wasn't for the fact that the service was in Ronald's name and that he was doing me a great favor by allowing me to have service through him, I probably would've let this bill go delinquent like so many of my other bills.

As time moved on, my phone being cut off became a recurring theme, and because of my vain attitude, this would have my patience growing thin. Who was I to even question Ronald when he was doing me a favor? With this happening more frequently, Ronald felt compelled to tell me the truth. He shared with me how long the grace period was and that sometimes he would just get the one phone interrupted until the third person would pay. This would leave me with the understanding that the entire balance didn't need to be paid in order to maintain having service. This was something I kept in the back of my mind.

I also noticed that Ronald never seemed to be upset with that person, so I naturally developed a more relaxed attitude when time came to pay the bill. If I had some urgent money matters at hand, I would just let Ronald know I would be late. I never allowed this to go beyond thirty days. Once we start paying our bills late, we all know how extremely hard it is to catch up. Ronald also shared with me that from time to time, he would use the bill money for other things with the idea that he would pay the bill before the deadline. Well, I believe you can understand where this was going. After doing this successfully a few times, this became the normal routine. We both were allowing the bill to go until we absolutely had to pay, me no longer than thirty days, and Ronald right before the deadline. This went on for months until finally something had to give.

Eventually, we started having more service interruptions. Now, I'm feeling like I didn't want my shortcomings to cause any more problems with our friendship. If I caused Ronald to have credit problems, he would never be able to forgive me, so I felt it was time for me to establish my own account. In order for me to do this and have the same number, the company needed his approval. In every attempt I made to do this, Ronald just dismissed it and reassured me that there would be no problems. One night, while we were together at my place, Ronald asked me if I would consider sharing an apartment with him. His idea was that this could help both of us out financially, and with our work schedules being the way they were, we would never be in each other's way. With my financial woes at the time, this was probably exactly what I needed, but my selfishness wouldn't allow me to even consider it. I also never stopped to think how this could possibly help out my best friend. All I thought about was I didn't want to share my space with someone, regardless of who it was. I also never thought about how my reaction to his proposal may have made him feel.

THE FRIENDSHIP WAS DAMAGED

Weeks went by after that short conversation about us sharing a place together. I was having some trouble with my car. After getting into a dispute with the service manager, I called Ronald to vent. Little did I know this conversation would lead to a defining moment in my life. I got Ronald on the phone and told him the service manager was telling me a lie about my car. I suggested he was trying to take advantage of me for more money. Ronald and I shared similar views, so whenever we faced a verbal confrontation with people throughout the course of the day, we would count on each other to bring confirmation about the way we would feel. There's nothing like having friends who listen and let us know we're not wrong for the way we feel. This helps calm your frustration. When I finished sharing to Ronald what happened, the conversation got nasty. Instead of lifting me up, or cosigning my point as we would call it, Ronald lashed out at me in a very nasty way. He said, "Take your car elsewhere if you feel like there's a conspiracy against you!" Those were his exact words, and in that moment, I became heated! Don't get me wrong, the statement was true, but it was the last thing I wanted to hear.

When I heard his words, my vanity would only allow me to see this as jealousy. I never thought about the way I dismissed his conversation weeks prior about us getting a place together. I thought Ronald, even though he didn't continually express his desire for us to do this, really wanted me to consider it. And the way I just brushed the idea off may have hurt his feelings and left him frustrated. At this point, he was definitely frustrated for some reason or another because now it was beginning to show. Through my anger, I said to him, "I was just calling you to vent, I didn't call to hear your sarcastic comments!" He quickly responded saying, "Why did you call me at all?" I knew then there was nothing left for us to talk about. In response, I set up my exit and said, "You won't ever have to worry about me calling you again." "Well, don't!" he replied. From there, we hung up the phone.

Going back to my vanity, I was thinking this all stemmed from the things I was doing in my life. At the time I thought because I had just purchased a Range Rover, which left me having two Range Rovers, and a pool table for my place, Ronald was feeling envious. So when I hung up the phone that day, I said to myself, "That motherf—! He's a jealous-hearted motherf—" I was so angry and upset, but looking at it now, what was making me so upset was the same thing that was causing the problems in the first place—my selfishness. I was so blinded by it that I couldn't see how insensitive I may have been to the things he may have been going through. Ronald wanted a place to stay. He asked me, and I brushed him off. He also may have been looking at me like I'm a person who didn't have any girl trouble, not knowing that I was only putting up a façade. You see, he may have been struggling within himself about his insecurities when it came to women. He was having trouble sustaining his relationships. The fact that we both loved playing pool (now I could play the game whenever I want, and I remember I would win most of the time when we played against each other) probably didn't help matters any. Think about it: who really wants to be around a person that things seem to be going well for, during a time when you feel things aren't going to well for you? This wasn't the case for me at all, but it's impossible for someone to see beyond what they perceive in regard to other people. I was struggling, and the choices I was making started to mount against me, but he had no idea of knowing this. If Ronald was feeling any of those things, I totally understood, but at the time, I wasn't in a place to see things clearly. What happened to our relationship would set the stage and leave me in a place searching for clarity. With this, I'm ever so grateful that it did.

FEELING EMPTY

The animosity between Ronald and me left little tolerance for the cell phone. The bill would soon become the breaking point for the relationship. It all started when I paid Ronald late for the April billing cycle. It was around the eighth of May, and two weeks later, I was surprised to find my cell phone was cut off. Immediately, I thought he did this out of spite. Because we weren't speaking, I thought he was paying me back by kicking me off the account. So now I decided to call the company once again to try to obtain my own service.

I had been paying this bill for years, so I felt the company would take that into consideration and allow me to have my own service. Speaking with the company, I realized I was eligible, but the only way I could keep the same number was through Ronald's permission. And I thought wow, now I had no choice but to call Ronald and talk to him. When I called him, his response was quick. Before I could say a word, he said, "Your phone is off because you didn't pay your bill." I was confused. I had just paid for April, and now the May payment wasn't that late, but nevertheless I was calling to try to get him to release the phone number. Ronald had the idea he would force me to give him money for the bill. I didn't believe the service was in cutoff status, so this led me to believe he was trying to use the service to obtain money for something else. I got this idea from having a conversation with my cousin, Leroy. He told me he received a strange text message from Ronald asking to borrow two hundred dollars. Ronald, of course, was unaware that the company would give me my own account, so I used that to get him to release the number. I had the edge in this situation, I still did owe Ronald for May's billing statement, and he was at a place where he needed to get his hands on some money. So I bargained with what I still owed. I told Ronald, I couldn't pay him if I had to use that money to get my own service. Getting a new number would require me to put money down, and to keep the same number I wouldn't have to do anything but just continue to pay the bill. So if he wanted me to pay for May, then he needed to release the number. At that point, I felt bad because I really wanted to talk to him about the whole thing, but I just didn't have the courage. He felt like he had no choice but to release the number, this way he would get the money he needed.

In the process, I deceived him; I gave him the impression I had the money that day, but instead of giving it to the service provider I would bring it to him. While we were on hold, Ronald made an effort to share some small talk. This was a sign he was trying to reach out, and this is where I failed him miserably as a friend. Knowing him so well, I knew he wanted to talk, but being so stuck in my ways, I continued to act like such a bastard. Soon, that behavior would come back to haunt me. After we ended the phone conversation with the service provider, everything was straightened out with my phone. It was then I decided to tell Ronald I wasn't going to pay him for May's payment until the following week. He got very quiet, some hesitation followed, and then he hung up the phone. I felt so bad, but not bad enough to do anything about our relationship.

What I was doing was still holding on to the bitterness I felt the day he got smart with me about my car. This was so stupid because I had a great friend in Ronald; his loyalty to our friendship was unmatched. I couldn't find a person as loyal as he is in all my friendships, so this was certainly something I should've been able to get beyond. The time came for me to meet up with him to pay what I owed. Originally I was going to pay him for the full month of May, but because of my bitterness, I decided to just pay him for the time up until the service was cut off. My behavior was too harsh; I could've, out of common courtesy, paid for the whole month since he helped me get the service in the first place.

THE LAST TIME I WOULD SEE HIM

When I met with Ronald to pay him the money, he surprised me when he said I owed him for two months. He suggested when I paid in April it was for March, and I still owed for April and May. Of course, my response was "You're crazy!"

I told him, "My bill was never two months behind. If it was that far behind, the service would've been interrupted long before the second week of May." In that moment, I felt so sad for him, but why didn't I take the opportunity to reach out and reconcile? We had so many years of friendship to let it end like this. Ronald looked at me as if he wanted to say something different, but his pride would only allow him to say "Man, I'm telling you, you owe me more money than this." He explained the billing cycle was always paid in advance. This didn't make much sense to me because I was convinced about the amount I owed, so I said to him, "Whatever. Not only do I not owe you that amount, but I'm only paying you for half of the month. From now on and the remainder of the month, the bill is in my name."

I gave him seventy dollars and got in my car and pulled off. Right now, as I write to you, my eyes are filled with tears because all I can see is that image of him standing there looking at me drive away. That was even more confirmation that he wanted to say more, but I continued to drive, acting very cold and harsh. The news that followed eight months later would make that scene become my last image of him. I had just lost a friend in Donnal, who was very dear to me, and was beginning to see some real truth about myself. Losing a friend with so much character can easily have you evaluating your own. The humbling experience that was needed for me to get past my pride and make things right with Ronald at this point didn't exist. And quite frankly, I now understand why; it wasn't supposed to.

I thought a lot about my relationship with Ronald. Often I wondered what he was doing and found myself missing the times we shared playing pool. In the back of my mind, I felt for some reason we would make things right again, and I couldn't wait because I wanted him to see my new place. My new place had so much more room for the pool table. I knew he would enjoy playing with me here, as opposed to where I used to live, so thoughts of us kicking it again were beginning to bring me excitement. I just knew the time would come for us to bury the hatchet, but the old lesson about not putting off tomorrow what you can do today would soon hit me like a ton of bricks.

One morning as I was getting ready for work, I received a phone call from my cousin, Manny. This was a phone call I wasn't expecting, but when I heard the somber sound of his voice, I instantly knew what the news would be. He asked me very quietly, "Did you hear about Ronald?" I cut him off as he was speaking and said, "No, please don't tell me that." But then he said, "Yeah, Ron passed away. My mom just shared the news with me this morning. She was wondering if you knew." At that point, things instantly became surreal. Unlike Donnal's passing, Ronald's would have me now reflecting on life in a whole new way. Donnal had taken ill and was hospitalized, and even though I got to a point where I thought he would pull through, there was still the possibility he would leave us. Ronald, on the other hand, wasn't speaking to me, so the news would take me totally by surprise.

Looking back on these two events, I realized they seemed to be commonly linked. Ronald was a heavy set guy who was gentle, a lot like Donnal. He too was a great friend to me through the years, and like Donnal, he also suffered from diabetes. I found myself saying the exact same things to them both and, in both cases, to no avail. I suggested they come and exercise with me, but neither one of them was ready nor got the chance to. This was so sad and such a humbling experience, but to me it was no coincidence. When Donnal passed away, I experienced a great revelation about life, but now after hearing this about Ronald, all I would be able to think about was my own immortality.

After Ronald's funeral, life felt strange. He had been absent from my life for the last eight months, but in my mind, he was always there. Now I would have to face the reality he was gone forever. At times, I just sat there saying to myself, "I can't believe he's gone!" I also thought, "What's going on in my life right now? People around me are dying. Will I be next?" For so long, I relished in the fact that I lived alone, but now this wasn't so good. I was really starting to feel lonely. I got the opportunity to talk with Ronald's mom at the funeral, and she shared the story of his last days. She didn't tell me the official cause of death, but she shared how he spent his last nights sleeping in a chair. He was having trouble with his stomach, and this was the only way he found comfort. She said, "When he came home from his last doctor visit, I asked him what the doctor said." His only response to her was, "He said I'm dying." From there, the conversation got quiet. There was nothing more to be said, and it made me imagine how alone he must have felt. In that moment, I wished I could've been there for him to maybe share a few laughs and offer some comfort, but now it was too late. I mentioned that I didn't believe what was happening in my life was a coincidence. Well, feeling this empty would only lead me to search for something to fill the void. This seemed very strategic as I watched the developments of my life in the months to come.

SEARCHING

I RECEIVED FOREWARNING

Word got around that Ronald had passed away. I went to work and was greeted in the hallway by my friend, Keith. Keith met Ronald on a few occasions, so he knew how close we were and for as long as I live, I don't think I will ever forget this moment. The moment Keith saw me, he instantly reacted as if something came over him with great urgency. In an instance, Keith became very animated, and for some reason he couldn't keep himself still. Pacing back and forth with his eyes wide open, he said to me, "Clayton! I don't know why I'm saying this, but I feel like I have to. Something is getting ready to happen to you! I don't know what, but God is getting ready to do something in your life, trust me on this! I can't tell you exactly what, but trust me." As he went on, he said, "Man! I'm telling you, Clayton, and it's going to be something really big." Keith put such authority and emphasis on his words. He never spoke to me quite like this before, and with the confidence he displayed, I had to pay attention.

At work, a lot of people misunderstand Keith. They liked to write him off as crazy. In my opinion, there was nothing crazy about him. On the contrary, Keith knew exactly what he was talking about. From the first time we met, we could relate to one another, and in time, I would see this too would serve great purpose.

MY SEARCH BEGINS

At work feeling bored and looking for something to fill the void, I decided to check my emails during my break. For years, I've been receiving emails from various friends about creating an account with a social network. I strongly felt I would never be a part of this, but I was so desperate to find something to do, so that day, I decided to entertain them. Quite honestly, I was also hoping in the back of my mind that this would lead to me meeting a new acquaintance.

Reluctantly, I created the account and have now become part of the network everyone is using. Little did I know, this was the beginning of a journey that would lead me to the greatest discovery of my life. Living my life blind to some things, I had no idea what I was saying when I answered a question during the account registration process. I was asked what my interests were and I answered "my daughter" and "discovering my life's purpose." What was made apparent as a result of that answer was the fact that I was trying to find myself. At the time, I didn't realize what I was really saying. I just thought the answer made me seem clever. We all know what happens when we look for something. It's like the old saying goes: you seek and you shall find. But I had no idea what was coming.

MY SECRET PAST

It was my senior year in high school, I was seventeen years old and I fathered a child. Just like any typical teenager, the last thing I was thinking about was taking on responsibility. No, what I was thinking about was all that life had in store for me. My girlfriend and I thought we were so in love, but we didn't have a clue what love was; we were just being guided by our hormones. When news of the pregnancy hit, we both became scared. My thinking was that this would ruin my dreams, and we both thought our first and only option was to have an abortion. We also thought we could have this without telling our mothers. According to her, her father would help her get an abortion, and with this plan in place, I felt for sure I wouldn't have to tell anyone about this situation. This marked the beginning of my secret past.

As I was trying to live a normal teenage life, fear of this situation kept rearing its ugly head. Instead of me enjoying the start of my senior year, I was spending my days thinking about this situation and hoping that it would be all over soon. Months went by, and the abortion hadn't taken place. Every time I asked about it, she would always tell me some story about her father failing to do one thing or another. Any answer she gave would satisfy me because

I really didn't want to be bothered with it. I just wanted the situation to go away and was leaving it to her to deal with as if she was the only one who laid down creating this so-called problem.

More time passed and you would think it would dawn on me that the abortion was probably not going to happen, and it didn't. The further along in the pregnancy you are, the more unlikely the chances are to have an abortion. But I just kept ignoring it, still hoping that it would be all over soon. In the meantime, she was doing such a good job at keeping this secret away from everyone.

She was getting bigger, and no one even noticed. I knew about the pregnancy, and even I couldn't tell. If I didn't witness this with my own eyes, I would find this story hard to believe. She was able to hide her pregnancy from everyone, including her mother, for the nine months she carried the baby. I thought it was incredible. I was still under the impression she was having an abortion because she told me there was a procedure that could be done, even though she was that far gone. So when she went to the hospital that day, I was under the assumption she was terminating the life, not having our baby. With that in mind, I felt relieved. Now I wouldn't have to tell my mother I got my girlfriend pregnant and have her thinking less of me. I love my mom, and all I wanted was for her to be proud of me. See, I was the youngest child, the one who gave her the most trouble. She had been through so much stress when it came to me, and the last thing I wanted was to put her through anymore. My thinking was, *After today, this situation will be over, and my secret would remain safe.* As the day went on, not being at the hospital made me grow anxious to hear about the situation, so I decided to call. When I called, I found out what room she was in, and the operator put me through. The anticipation was really mounting, and I couldn't wait to hear her tell me it was all over.

The phone rang a few times, then suddenly I heard a voice say, "Hello," but it wasn't my girlfriend. To my surprise, her mom was there and she answered the phone. Even though we were on the phone, I could still see the expression of anger on her face as she said to me "Clayton, why did you and my daughter lie to me all this time about her being pregnant?" I didn't have an answer. "I am very disgusted with you and her," she said, and then I heard silence until my girl's voice came on the line, "Hello," she said. I said to her, "Is everything okay? Did something go wrong?" I couldn't understand why her mother was there at the hospital with her. She said very softly to me, "Everything is okay," and then she got quiet. Her silence made it clear because all of a sudden I realized she didn't terminate the life; instead, she had the baby. At that moment, I couldn't feel anything but fear. Through my fear, I reluctantly asked, "Did you have the baby?" She replied, "Yeah," and then I said, "What is it, a boy or a girl?" her response was "A boy, and I named him Marcus Clayton Jones." From there, I got silent and all I can remember was ending the phone conversation telling her everything would be okay.

To be perfectly honest, I wasn't so sure of that; I was scared. I found myself in a position where I had to deal with my truth. I could no longer hide this from my mother, and I was anticipating feeling the wrath of her anger. I thought she would be so disgusted with me that our relationship would be over. Even if I wasn't still under her care, this was a relationship I didn't want to lose. This was the one constant love I had in my life. Standing in front of my mom ready to deliver the news, I thought to myself, *I can't believe all of this is happening. Why now, why me? I don't want her looking at me through the eyes of disappointment.* Also, I wasn't just going to tell her my girlfriend was pregnant. I was also going to tell her I kept this secret from her, and that now she would be a grandmother too.

I had to confess two very serious things at once, and what made matters worse was the feeling I had that my hands were tied leaving me no choice. The time came for me to say it, I was hesitant, afraid, and did not know how I was going to bring myself to say the words. Then out of nowhere for a split second the fear subsided, allowing me to state the truth. "Ma, I got a son. My girlfriend didn't tell me she was pregnant, and I'm just finding out now I have a baby." Very angrily, she said, "What?" I said, "Yeah, my girlfriend didn't tell me she was pregnant. She hid it from me and her mother, and as a matter of fact, she hid it from everyone. We're just finding out now." Some truth I told.

What a coward I was. Instead of standing up like a man, I was willing to let my girlfriend take more of the blame than she deserved. My mother looked at me in disgust. She was mad as hell, but not nearly as mad as I thought she would be. Maybe it was because I didn't give her the whole truth. She expressed being very disappointed in both of us and couldn't believe my girlfriend would do something like this. After a frustrating sigh, all she said was "Clayton, we'll just have to do the best we can with raising this child." What else could she really say at that point? I was really hurt by the fact I let her down. It wasn't long after, that the truth about me knowing all along my girlfriend was pregnant came out. And on December 29, 1987, a secret that would forever change my life was born into the world.

I WASN'T READY

When my child arrived, all I had was a part-time job on the weekends, and I relied on my mother for everything. Being the youngest of three, I was spoiled and I was used to getting a lot of things I wanted. With this situation, however, I could no longer rely on her. I was being propelled into adulthood, which left me no time to be a child. I thought this to be so unfair. Why did I have to be the one that became a statistic? I just wanted to live my life and chase my dreams. Was that too much to ask? The hardest thing for me to resist would be the desire to get what I wanted out of life. How would I be able to overcome this? I felt like I couldn't!

Being in high school didn't help matters much; it made it exceedingly difficult for both of us to stay focused on our relationship. My relationship with her at the time felt like my lifeline. All I thought about was not losing her. I often thought of this more than being a father to my son.

As a result of some cheating I did while playing high school basketball and spending the little bit of money I was making from my job on myself, I felt for sure I would lose her. The one important thing I was overlooking was the role my relationship with my son would play in my desire to keep her. If I wasn't ready to be a father to her son, what made me think any of these other things would even matter? Being a father was the most important variable, but I was too young to understand that.

THE INEVITABLE

I mentioned this before: Being a teenage boy, how could I resist the temptation of my dreams? I couldn't. I didn't understand any other joy but the joy of being able to keep up with my peers. I loved being able to stay current with the latest fashion and have people look at me like I was down. Also, the biggest misconception I wanted to keep alive was that the baby wasn't going to change a thing in my life. Everyone else's future was bright, and so was mine. I wasn't going to let people look at my circumstances any different. This was such foolishness on my part, and I would eventually pay a heavy price for learning the lesson.

My girlfriend was steadily losing faith in me, and I felt like I was losing her fast. The lack of effort I was putting into fatherhood and the insecurities I displayed within the relationship were pushing her further away from me and into the arms of another. Feeling her slipping from my grasp, I made two attempts to maintain the relationship. The most significant attempt was the Senior Prom. I didn't have the desire or the resources to go to the prom, but at the last moment she wanted to go, so in an effort to make her happy, I found a way. We had a great time, and the desire to keep her in my life intensified. I remembered thinking to myself while looking at her in the car, *Man I love her so much, and I have to make the necessary sacrifices for her and my son.* The feelings were so strong for me that night, it made me believe in my heart that I was ready to make changes.

After the prom, I found myself aggressively pursuing spending more time with her and the baby. Of course, she allowed this; all she wanted from me in the first place was to be there for my son. In the midst of feeling like I wanted to make things right, I had no idea she was hiding yet another secret. After going to our senior class trip and the prom together, wherein we had a great time and expressed our love for one another, she decided to drop a bomb on me I had a hard time recovering from. My idea of trying to recover from it was to run away and look for comfort. I stated earlier I could sense something was wrong, but I never thought it would be this.

One night, a few days after the prom, I was at her house spending time. I was talking to her about our relationship and all the while, she was non-responsive. In the past, these things I shared were exactly what she liked to hear, but now, it was as if she could care less. Of course, this led to an argument, and out of frustration, I started saying things I didn't mean but certainly felt at the time. In the midst of our argument, she did the unthinkable. She picked up the phone and called another guy right in front of me. I couldn't believe what I was seeing. I sat there so stunned I couldn't react. Listening to the conversation, I knew they both had been seeing each other for some time, and with this I was finally made aware of the fact she was moving on. It felt like my world came crashing down. I immediately called my brother to come get me out of there and started cussing her out. "You, bitch! How you gonna disrespect me and call another nigga right in front of my face?" I could hear the nigga yelling over the phone, and all she did was sit there, with a sneaky ass smile on her face, ignoring me. I said, "Imma get you back for this, you watch. You watch and see!"

I had to get as far away from her as I could. I was so hurt. I left her house feeling like I never wanted to see her again. I couldn't handle anything that reminded me of her, including my son, so I stayed away leaving her to shoulder all the responsibility of taking care of our baby. I became so bitter, and little did I know, this was what she wanted all along, so the only person I was hurting was myself. This event marked the end of my relationship with her and my son and would give birth to yet another secret we both would try to suppress in different ways. I would try to live my life like I didn't have a son, and she would try to live her life like someone else was his father.

MOVING ON

During this period of my life, everyone who knew me knew I fathered a child, so the secret would only be for those I would encounter moving forward. I also met Rhonda during that time, so she was aware of my son as well. I would always be reminded by my family and through dreams that he was there. Also, when Rhonda and I officially became a couple, she would always encourage me to look for him. Rhonda never let me forget about my son, sometimes I felt like she wanted to be a part of his life more than I did. This was one of the things I loved so much about her, and eventually, she and I would bring a beautiful baby into this world of our own. So on September 20, 1994, our bond was forever cemented with the birth of our baby girl, Jazmin Monae Jones.

As Jazmin grew, we both made sure she knew she had a brother. We didn't want anything unfortunate to happen because we all know how small this world can be. This was one secret I refused to keep from her. Knowing this and her being the only child, it was only natural for her to develop a desire to want to meet and also be around her big brother. I think there's an instinctive feeling you get toward a sibling, especially when that sibling is older than you. From time to time, she would make comments about how she wished she had a brother or sister, and when she got old enough, she would even ask me about finding my son. So as you can see, my past had its own journey, and that journey followed me as I traveled throughout life.

As time went on, there were instances where family members ran across my son and his mother. This was evidence that she couldn't ever escape her past or suppress her truth either. It was as if this secret we were keeping was haunting us both. My son believed the man raising him was his father. His mother was doing everything in her power to not let the truth come out and feeling like raising him this way was for the best. As time moved on, I found out she unofficially changed his name to further perpetuate this lie. This would cause problems when it came to him attending school. The birth certificate was never changed, so the school records had his official name. When his teachers would call him by the last name Jones, it created confusion and curiosity within him. Over the years, that curiosity would lead him to ask questions in his mind, and he couldn't help but wonder why this kept happening. It was a reason she never got around to changing his birth certificate. That reason would be revealed and it had nothing to do with her procrastinating.

IT WOULDN'T GO AWAY

When my son grew to be thirteen years old, I got a surprise. One day, my uncle William (God rest his soul) bumped into my son's mom in the grocery store. Immediately when he saw her, the situation came to mind. He asked her how everything was going and if he could have her phone number so they could keep in touch. Surprisingly, she said yes, and from there, he asked a question that suggested his intention. "You know what I'm going to do with the phone number, right?" She said, "Yeah, I know." My uncle smiled and thanked her, then gave her a hug. He felt for certain he was doing a great deed but had no idea I really didn't want him doing this. I was afraid of confronting my truth and had grown pretty comfortable with living as if I had only one child. Everyone I worked with, and even my new friends, thought that I only had a daughter, I didn't want anyone looking at me as a person who doesn't have a relationship with his child, so, as you can see, this wasn't something I was too thrilled about.

As he gave me the phone number, he told me the story. I felt like I couldn't have him thinking I wasn't interested in seeing my son, so I showed great appreciation though deep inside I didn't want to make the call. I knew he would tell everyone in the family he gave me her number, so again

I felt like I had no choice. To me, it's like facing the bully on the block, your family is standing behind you, and you don't want to let them down. You feel at this point there is nowhere for you to run, so you have to face the consequences one way or another. Deal with my family or deal with my fear, and at this point, the fear of having my family look at me in that light was greater. So I decided to call.

The one thing we fear the most is the unknown, and not knowing what to expect when I called, you can only imagine what I was feeling. I thought to myself, *Do I really want another responsibility in my life at this point*? I was already struggling to take care of the one I had. But out of obligation and the feeling that this was the right thing to do, I went through with it. I called her, and she answered. Then for fear the conversation would be awkward, and with no other words I could find, I quickly said, "How are you?" She said, "I'm fine, are you married yet?" I thought this was peculiar, but quite honestly I was flattered, so I said, "No, not yet, but what about you?" She said, "No." From there, I grew comfortable with the conversation and realized things weren't going to be so bad, after all.

I began speaking openly about the past and where my life was currently. I shared with her that I knew she had a daughter with the same name as my daughter's, and I thought it was important our son knew he had another sister. I also expressed I thought they should meet. I wanted to move on from the past, I felt strongly I was over all the things that happened before and was only interested in how we could make things right from this point on. I said to her, "I appreciated them both for the job they've done so far, and now it was time for us to come together and do the right thing."

After digesting what I said, she expressed something, which allowed me to continue my life as if I had one child. "I don't think it's a good idea to tell him who you are. All this time, he's believed one thing, and learning the truth now will only ruin his life. You can see him, but you can't say anything." My reply was, "What am I supposed to say about who I am? That's crazy. I'm not going to lie to my son." She replied, "Well, I'm not going to allow you to see him." And on that note, we hung up.

To be honest, I was relieved in a sense because now I had built an excuse for my family and I could say I was no longer to blame. I reached out, and she wanted me to lie; everyone would understand why I declined this proposal. This was perfect, but deep down I was still hiding my truth. If I really wanted to see my son, I could've gone along with what she suggested, and done whatever I felt once I saw him. Love for your kids will have you jumping over all hurdles, especially if it's to make them a part of your life. Don't misunderstand, deep inside I did want him to be a part of my life, but what was made obvious to me was that my fear about this situation was greater. So instead of facing that fear, I was just fine with the way things were.

After that last conversation, I thought this situation was settled for good. I further moved on with my life thinking I probably won't be confronted by this truth ever again. Until one day three years later, I received a phone call from my sister, Denise. Her son, Eric, came home from school with some news. Eric remembered I, his Uncle Clayton, had a son named Marcus. The news was there was a boy in his class who looked just like me and who also happened to be named Marcus. My sister got excited and sent Eric to school with some questions she wanted him to ask Marcus. She knew it was her long-lost nephew, but she wanted to make certain. She told Eric to ask Marcus what his mom's name was and if his mom knew who Eric and Chanae (Eric's sister) were. Through a process, everything got confirmed, and all of a sudden the truth could no longer be hidden.

Once my nephew started asking questions, the conversation gave Marcus the desire to find out what Eric was talking about. From there, my son found out I was his father. One day, he came to school and said to Eric, "What's up, cuz?" Eric was completely surprised, then Marcus said, "Yeah, I know everything. I know we're family." Eric smiled, and their bond grew closer from that point. Eventually, this would lead to me receiving a phone call that would bring me into question.

My sister called me without hesitation, and I answered the phone. She said, "Clayton, guess what? Eric is in the same class with Marcus." I said. "For real?" She replied, "Yup, they're in the same class. Hold on, I'm going to let you talk to Eric." My fear became greater than before, I felt like people were pushing me to confront what I was running from. I could also see this wasn't going away. I was so nervous about what I might be facing, and it felt like it was a force that just wouldn't allow me to totally abandon this situation. It was as if something was saying to me, "You're not getting off that easy."

I can remember when Eric picked up the phone, I said, "Tell me what he's like." Eric really didn't give much, he just said, "Man, he looks just like you and his mother mixed together. And he's mad cool." I also asked, "What did you tell him about me?" "I told him you were cool, and you two were a lot alike." "Oh, okay." Far from being over with my fear of this situation, I told Eric "Give him my number. I don't know how he feels, so I'll let him call me when he's ready." Being consumed with the perception I thought people would have of me, I felt I had to do something.

If I really wanted to see my son, I could've gone to the school, but it was obvious I wasn't ready for him to be a part of my life. At this point, I was no longer with Rhonda and was living alone and struggling to recover from the financial burdens I brought upon myself through my addictions. My thinking was, *If he's in my life right now, I'll need to be able to afford him. I wanted to see clear of my financial situation first.* Who was I fooling? It never works out that way and money can never make up for what really got lost in time. No; this was just a weak attempt to re-unite with my son. I knew he wouldn't call; I just wanted to be free from the opinion I didn't want my son in my life.

MY CURIOSITY

I wasn't the only one running from this truth. After my son developed an understanding that I was his father and that he had a family out there excited about meeting him, his mom decided to make her next move. In an effort to avoid the inevitable, at the end of the year she decided to remove him from the school. This forced him and Eric to lose contact and decreased the chance for us to ever meet. When Eric told me Marcus was no longer at his school, again I thought it was over. I hid how I truly felt behind the things his mom did, hoping people would believe I wanted desperately for him to be a part of my life and that it was her keeping him from me. Again, this provided me the perfect situation, so I wouldn't have to face my truth.

MY DAUGHTER WANTED
TO KNOW HER BROTHER

One of the best things I did as a father was to make sure Jazmin knew she had a brother. This never left her mind, and being the only child, she longed to have a sibling. Jazmin seemed to envy some of her friends who had siblings and expressed a desire for me to get married and have a brother or sister for her to play with. She always felt alone at family gatherings, and the desire, until it was addressed, would only grow greater. Without having to express how much, I knew my daughter wanted badly to know her brother.

Moving back to the present, living alone and experiencing the sudden death of both Donnal and Ronald, I was feeling like life was changing and I didn't have much to look forward to. Then one day, while playing around on the network, a great idea popped into my head. The idea was to see if I could find my son's pictures. Marcus was twenty-two years old, and, chances were, he was probably on social networks like all other young adults his age. So being bored and curious about what he might look like, I decided to search his name.

As I typed his name in the search box, everything around me felt surreal. I remember feeling nervous, as if we were coming face-to-face. By no means did I want to reach out, so chances were, I never would've sent him a friend request. These things normally take a few seconds, but at the time, it felt more like minutes. Waiting for a response, I wondered what he was going to look like, and then suddenly it happened. Some names popped up matching my search. *After all these years, I'll finally get the chance to see my son, even if just from a safe distance*, I thought.

My anticipation was at its highest point as I clicked on the profile that showed a person from Baltimore. To my surprise, a little girl's picture showed up. Frantically, my eyes began scanning the page for a male's picture. I searched and searched until finally I came across the name of his sibling listed on his page. Lo and behold, the name of his sister was the same as my daughter's, and I thought this couldn't be a coincidence. I remembered talking to his mom about us having daughters with the same name, so this person was a direct match to my son. I knew it was him. Not only did I know all that I had known from logically processing, I could also feel it. When we reproduce life, there's an internal bond created, a bond that we're unable to break. With these feelings, my desire to see what he looked like was intensified. While on the page, I tried to access his photos, but it wouldn't allow me unless I was his friend. For now, I would just be left with the anxiety and curiosity of wanting to see pictures of my son.

WHY DID I TELL
MY DAUGHTER

As I stated before, it seemed as if there was a force behind what was happening, and now it wasn't allowing me the luxury of being able to see my son from a distance. It felt like this force was going to make me go further than I wanted to. Without thinking, I got off the internet and immediately called my daughter to tell her the news. I couldn't believe this, I was so close to seeing my son. When I spoke with my daughter, I specifically said to her, "Jaz, I believe I found Marcus on the network. I'm not completely sure it's him. It's his name, but there's a picture of a little girl. Before I do anything, I'm going to wait to see if the picture changes to make sure," My daughter replied, "For real, Daddy?" I said, "Yeah, so don't do anything. Let me handle this." She replied, "Okay, I won't."

The reason I said this was because of my intentions at the time. I was running from the truth about a lot of things in my life. I had recently closed a bank account because creditors were accessing my funds before I had a chance to get my hands on any, and I also conveniently relocated because I was too behind on my rent to ever get caught up. So the last thing I thought I had the strength to do was face this truth that had been haunting me for the last twenty years. All I wanted was to see my son from a safe distance, so this is why I asked my daughter not to do anything.

If I had been thinking clearly I would've realized there was no way this would ever work. If I was excited about seeing what he looked like, I could only imagine what was on her mind. This happened on a Friday evening. I was headed home to spend another uneventful weekend hoping to be able to see past the void I was suffering from. Realizing my son was just a click away would serve as a great distraction from my reality. All I could think about that night was him, but it would be short-lived because I had just worked a twelve-hour shift. Being tired from work, it didn't take much for me to fall asleep.

The next day while at work, I received an unexpected phone call from Rhonda. I instantly thought she wanted to ask me to pick Jaz up for the day. Whenever I received phone calls on Saturdays from her, it was always to give me grief about her not getting a break from my daughter. Well, I was reluctant to answer the phone because I really wasn't in the mood to hear her complain about what she thought I should be doing. This time though, her reason for calling was very different. When I answered the phone, she started the conversation by asking me this question, "Hey, did you tell Jaz about Marcus being on the network?" I paused, and my thinking was, *Oh boy, what did she do*. I said, "Yeah, I told her about it. Why?" "Well, I just wanted to let you know that those two are friends now. He told her he wants to meet up with her and take her to the movies. He also told her he would call sometime today. I suggested she send a friend request and when she did, he accepted. I sent a message to him as if I was her, telling him I was his sister. His response was 'how?' and I said "I'm your father's daughter." Then his response was "Does he know about me?" I told him, "Yes, he does."

When she finished explaining everything, all the fear I had regarding this situation felt like it had overtaken me and turned into fury. At the top of my lungs, I yelled into the phone, "Why the hell are you always in my business? These are my kids and this is my situation! I specifically told Jaz not to do anything! I told her I would handle this myself and you get on my f— nerves. You're always worrying about me and what I'm doing! Stay the f— out of my business! Damn, you're always in my f— business!" Rhonda quickly responded with "Whatever. I don't care how you feel, she needs to know her brother. He seems like he's been looking for you all. I get the sense he's ready, and he wants to meet his family."

I couldn't say anything to that. From there, I knew I had to deal with my fear. I felt like things were being forced on me, and there was nothing I could do. I was really feeling afraid of what he might think of me and the reality that he could possibly reject me. I hung up the phone, went outside and sat in my car, evaluating this situation. Whenever we're faced with fear, we look for a safe haven. What came to mind was to do what I've always done, so I called my mother. By just being able to hear her voice and know that she was there, she seemed to be able to always comfort me about any situation. When I talked to my mom and shared the news, she was able to calm me down, and at the same time she couldn't believe what was happening. I had no idea when this would come to a head, but at this point, I was sure it would. I got off the phone and began envisioning what the interaction would be like when my son and I would finally come face to face.

EXPECTING THE WORST

O ver the years, I periodically gave thought to what it would be like if my son and I ever had the chance to re-unite. Picturing this in my mind, I always imagined the worst case scenario. I felt like the way his mom felt toward me would be his only influence, and rejecting me was the obvious response I would get. I also thought about the way things were in the black community and figured he would be similar to other young men his age who didn't know their biological father. The mentality is a "f— you" mentality. I could picture him blowing me off saying, "You haven't been here for me my whole life, so why come around now? I don't need or want anything from you! Get out of my face. You're not my father!"

The thought of this only perpetuated more fear, so that Saturday afternoon when I got off of work, I found myself consumed in it. The inevitable was going to happen, and there was nothing I could do about it. That afternoon while driving home, I received a call from my daughter asking me if I could come pick her up. This was a little strange. Normally if our weekends weren't planned prior to, it would be her mother who would call with the request. My first thought was, what is she up to now? Nevertheless, I agreed to pick her up and told her I would see her in a little while.

I took care of a few things that afternoon and finally I was with my daughter. The whole time we were in the car, I could feel her wanting to ask me something about the situation. She knew her mother and I had a discussion earlier, and she was dying for me to bring it up. I wasn't going to, and to be perfectly honest, because of the fear I felt, I was still wishing for this to go away. During the drive and throughout the day, I remained silent on the subject, and eventually this drove her to the point where she couldn't take it anymore. Sitting across from me while watching television, she broke the silence. My daughter turned to me and said, "Dad, don't you wanna know?" I said, "Know what, Jaz?" "About the boy," (I believed she was uncomfortable calling him my son). I said, "Of course, I do." "Well, why aren't you saying anything?" I told Jaz I had nothing to say and that if she wanted to discuss him, then she should just do it and not wait for me to bring it up.

The tension was eased a little, so she asked if I wanted to see what he looked like. I jumped at the chance to see his pictures because this was what I wanted in the first place. As I placed myself beside her on the couch, she scrolled through her friend's list on the network until she arrived at my son's page. In my mind, I was thinking, this is it! Again, I was so nervous. After all these years, I was finally getting the chance to see my son. And then it happened. My daughter, with that cute smile on her face, passed the phone to me. In that moment, I experienced something I never had the chance to experience before. Looking at the first picture of my son, I could see a younger version of me. There was no difference between him and me when I was his age, the likeness was almost identical. I was in awe and, in that moment, I felt like I was witnessing something miraculous. I could see myself reproduced in the physical form, and it existed on earth at the same time I did. Seeing his pictures took me into a deeper thought, *how could this be? This person was me all over again.* This process was so amazing, and all I wanted to do was find out more.

Even though I had my daughter to watch grow, I realized this was so different. I was a man, and my son was a replica of me; he was my sequel. I could never get this understanding I was developing now with my daughter, regardless of how much she looked like me. My daughter was a woman, so she could never be me. With my son being absent from my life, this was the very thing I needed for me to realize, or even think, about life differently. This would create a feeling inside of me that I couldn't understand at the time, but would make me analyze life so much deeper in the days to come.

With every picture, the feelings intensified. Every pose he made for the camera was showing me different facets of him. As I watched, I could visualize what he may have been thinking while the picture was being taken. I found myself saying, "That's exactly the way I would've posed for that picture!" This was so jaw-dropping! Fathers get to experience this by watching their sons grow in real life. Although not the same, this still had the same effect on me as I looked on. Everything around me became nonexistent, I was unaware of anything, and the moment had me feeling like it was a dream. I was in deep concentration focusing on the pictures when suddenly the phone rang. When she heard the phone, my daughter looked at the number and, in a panic, said, "Daddy, it's him. What do I do?"

"Oh my God, right while we were looking at his pictures and discussing him, he calls!" My daughter's hands began to shake. Suddenly, she lost all confidence to pick up the phone. I said to my daughter, "Calm down and answer the phone."

"What will I say?" she said. I told Jaz to just say hello. Honestly speaking, I really didn't know what to say either, but I knew with everything there is a beginning. Suddenly, while this was happening, my body was overtaken by the butterflies that started in my stomach. My entire body had this feeling, and at that point I also started to lose all thought. I went blank for what seemed like minutes, and what made me snap out of it was hearing my daughter say hello.

From there, things became very awkward for all of us. My daughter was so nervous that her speech was quickened; she needed to take a deep breath. She walked into the other room with the phone because she couldn't stand still. I remained sitting in my recliner listening to her conversation closely and hoping I could pick up on the sound of his voice. I thought this would possibly give me a feel for his vibe. As I listened, I heard my daughter say, "I'm with my Dad now. Would you like to talk to him?" *Oh boy, the time has come*, I thought, and all I can remember from that moment was her giving me the phone. After that, everything around me slowed down. It was like the world stopped for a moment. The television was on, but I couldn't hear it and my mind had really drawn a blank. If not for subconsciously being directed from all the years of answering the telephone, I would've had no words to say. We'd done this so many times before, so the right word came to me to break the ice. The same rules that applied for my daughter applied for me; the word that came to me to say was "hello."

This moment was indescribable. I felt completely numb, like I had been detached from my flesh. When he said "hello," his voice was so deep it made me feel a little intimidated. I began to speak, and my speech was quickened just like my daughter's, and in a hurry I said to him, "I really don't know what to say. I don't want to dwell on the past because we can't change it, but if there's anything you would like to know, I'll tell you. I can only tell you the part I played because I can't speak for anyone else, and I feel like I owe it to you to tell you the truth." I also went on to say, "Where are you now? And is it okay for me and Jaz to come pick you up so we can all spend some time together?" With no hesitation, he said, "Sure, why not?"

It was such a relief. I became convinced things weren't going to be as bad as I thought. Up until this point, all I could do was imagine the worst. Internally, I began to calm down, but I didn't hesitate to get my things together and rush out the door. When I left work that day, I had no idea later that night I would be on my way to meet my son. It's funny how in just a split second, your whole life can change. My son was living with his grandmother, and this too was a relief because I'm not sure I would've been able to face his mom. When we arrived at his house, I had such mixed emotions. I was feeling a combination of joy, excitement, and nervousness all at once. The one thing that helped me overcome my feelings was the overwhelming feeling of gratitude. I became extremely grateful this reunion was being forced on me.

When we entered the house, I received yet another surprise because his grandmother greeted me with a smile and a hug. She was just as grateful about this whole thing happening as I was. The hug I received from her gave me one of the best feelings I've ever experienced in my life. I felt forgiveness being relayed through the embrace. I loved this feeling, and it was probably the first time I really paid attention to it in this way. But from that point forward, I would always be able to recognize it when I feel it.

We exchanged pleasantries, I introduced my daughter and spoke on how all this was such a blessing, from there, my focus shifted to my son's bedroom door. I took a seat and began staring at the door while getting myself ready for the ultimate moment of truth. The anticipation in me really mounted, and I started thinking to myself, *I can't take this anymore*. And then it happened. The door opened, and the time finally came for me to narrow down all the different ways I had rehearsed on how I would greet him for the first time. *Which one should I choose?* My mind drew a blank again, but I shortly realized I still had time. When he opened the door, he came out only to go into the bathroom, so the greeting was put on hold. All I got at that point was a quick glimpse of him before he was out of sight. *Man, I wish this would happen already!* With my head held down and feeling the anticipation really getting to me, I suddenly looked up, and there he was, headed directly toward me. This happened so fast that I didn't have time to think; all I could do was react.

MY SON AND I COME FACE-TO-FACE

I stood up to greet my son, and this moment felt incredibly awkward. Imagine coming face-to-face with your child, and your child does not know what he or she should refer to you as. Natural instincts took over, and he gave me a hand shake with a hug, like brothers do when they greet each other on the street. With his extremely deep voice, he said to me, "Hey, what's up?" At that moment, all that mattered was that he was willing to greet me at all.

I smiled at him and said, "Nothing much. How are you?" The conversation became a blur because all I could focus on was the feeling or the sensation that overwhelmed me in that moment. I was so relieved, so at peace, and so overjoyed. All I wanted to do was hurry up and get him out of there, so we could spend some time alone. I was glad my daughter was there for them two to meet, but what I really wanted was for him and me to be alone. Once we left his house, my mind began racing, thinking about where I should take him first. Of course, this dilemma would only last for a split second. It only made sense to take him to that one place I truly call home. It was a must that I take him to my mother's house. I believed this reunion shouldn't and couldn't be delayed until morning.

MY MOM'S GIFT

When we got in the car, I was overflowing with excitement. I couldn't resist the urge to pick up the phone and call my mother. The first thing we do when something exciting or not so exciting happens is gravitate to our foundation. I wanted to surprise her with this precious gift, and it was going to take all the strength I had to keep from spoiling the surprise. I really wanted to pick up the phone and call, but I resisted because all I could think about was seeing the look on her face when she finally got the chance to see her grandson.

When I reached my mom's street, I decided to call. She answered the phone, and I couldn't help but sound excited. I managed to tell her very little in the exchange. I simply said, "Were you sleeping? If so, I'm sorry to wake you." To be perfectly honest, I didn't care about waking her up because to me this was big! Then she said, "That's all right. What's wrong?" "Nothing is wrong. I have a little surprise for you and Al (my mother's husband). Can you come downstairs and open the door?" By this time, I was just seconds away from my mother's house. When I parked the car and made my way to the house, all I could see was the porch light shining down on us. The light was so bright it made it hard to see who was standing at the door. This gave me the feeling like the news cameras was there, and the world was watching, awaiting eagerly for this reunion.

The moment was so significant to me because all these years my mom went above and beyond to help me. Over the years, I felt like there was nothing I could give her to make up for all the sacrifices she's made. But now, I was going to deliver to her the greatest gift I could possibly give—her grandson. A grandson whom, I believe, she may have given up hope on ever seeing. This would be a gift that would far surpass any disappointment I may have caused her throughout my life. This was the ultimate gift, and knowing this, I was filled with so much joy. I was so happy I couldn't stop smiling in that moment, even if I tried.

We were out of the car and made our way up the steps still blinded by the light. All the while, I was thinking to myself, *This is it!* My mom was going to be so happy to see Marcus, and at the same time, she probably wouldn't believe what she was about to see. I was filled with so much excitement, and, finally making it up the stairs onto the porch, we crossed over the threshold of the front door. I walked in first, blocking her view and trying to prolong the surprise. And then it happened. I said to my mom, "I have somebody I want you to meet." I turned to introduce my son, and before I could make the introduction, she said, "Oh, my God! Marcus?" My mother reached up and hugged him so tightly, a hug that seemed to last for minutes. After the long embrace, she put her hands to his face, touching it, as if she wanted to make sure it was really him. That moment was indescribable, so I don't know why I'm even trying to describe it.

My mother kept touching his face, and everything else in the room didn't exist because my focus was so tightly fixated on them. My mom's eyes filled with tears, and her face had a smile that was brighter than the porch light that shined down on us. My mom was glowing, and this glow was the same glow a woman has when she is impregnated with new life. It was like there was an illuminating light within her and radiating so strongly it shined right through the flesh, thus creating the appearance of a glow. I believe the presence of my son was creating a sense of new life for all of us. The burdens of past mistakes were heavy on our hearts, and this reunion symbolized the weight of those burdens being lifted. Once these burdens are lifted, you get the sense of the slate being wiped clean, hence the thought of a new beginning. My mom had the look on her face of a person who felt the relief that comes from holding a breath too long, and now we were finally able to breathe. Now she could see the type of young man he had grown to be without having to imagine or visualize it through her dreams. This was the best gift I could give, and it made me feel so content with my life in that instance. I was ready to face this situation like a man, so it could bring my mother's family back together.

My mother had experienced great loss in recent years with the death of my grandmother, my Aunt Virginia, my Uncle William, her stepfather Dennis, and my aunt Joyce suffering from Alzheimer's. At times, I could see it had taken its toll on her, and now the very thing we take for granted, which is family, would be the very thing that would give her a sense of wholeness again. All these years, I searched my mind thinking about what to give her on special occasions. Never once did it occur to me that seeing her grandson would be the perfect gift. This is the kind of gift that keeps on giving and has the ability to bring everlasting joy.

My mom was so happy, and, after coming back down to reality, she made plans for us to come over in the morning. She wanted to have Sunday breakfast with her children and grandchildren present. The idea was the natural thing to do. This would give us all the chance to sit, talk, and create some new family memories.

I COULDN'T SLEEP

After we left my mom's, I made two brief stops. I had to take my son to see my brother Raymond and my sister Denise, and then my children and I headed home. Back at the house, we spent almost the entire night talking. My son made me feel like all was forgiven, and his maturity about the matter was mind blowing. I was at a place in my life where I was beginning to realize all things happen for a reason, but to hear him say this was so much more powerful.

Throughout the course of the night, the more he talked, the stronger the feeling became that I had actually reproduced myself. I never got the chance to analyze the reproduction process in this way, and man, he was saying things exactly the way I would. As I was trying to think of all the things I ever wanted to say to him, I found myself running out of things to say, so I decided to go in my room to get some sleep. As I was trying to go to sleep, I found myself walking back and forth from room to room. I was restless and enjoying the opportunity to stare at both of my kids. A few minutes passed, and there I was again tossing and turning, and getting up out of my bed, until Marcus found words to put me at ease.

Over the years, I had dreams of chasing his mother while she was carrying him in her arms, and every time I got close enough to reach them, she would escape by getting on the bus. I believe the dream was a representation of my fears. The fear was if I didn't stand up soon and be a man, there was a chance I would never see my son again. What Marcus got compelled to say to me in that moment were the perfect words a father like me needed to hear. What he said was "You can go in the room and get some sleep. I'm not going anywhere. When you wake up, I'll be here." What a gift that was. I'm thinking, *If only I could pull you all inside of me to have you see exactly the way it made me feel.*

For the first time since he was a baby, I finally felt like I had a son. Marcus managed to ease my mind, but it still didn't put me to sleep. I was like a kid on Christmas Eve, the excitement about what was to come just wouldn't allow my eyes to close. Eventually, my body shut down forcing me to sleep.

The next morning, I woke up to the sight of both my kids, and I thought, *Good, it wasn't a dream. From there, I was ready to start what I felt would be the perfect day.*

THE PERFECT DAY

The sun appeared brighter than ever, my kids were with me, and my daughter was feeling great about not being the only child. My mom was preparing a big breakfast for her children and grandchildren. It was Sunday morning, and this was how things were supposed to be. It had been a long time coming, and, now that it was here, it was worth everything it took to make it happen. We ate breakfast, and phone calls were made, letting the whole family know about Marcus. Although family didn't come join us, it did inspire us to make plans to have a family gathering where everyone would get the chance to meet and welcome Marcus. In the meantime, we enjoyed the moment by taking pictures, laughing and asking questions, and everyone seemed to have what they wanted. You would think my son would feel awkward, but on the contrary, he had his homeboy with him, my nephew Eric. All in all, it was a day filled with emotions, and I found myself shedding tears of joy.

WHO ELSE COULD IT BE

The day was drawing to an end. My daughter had gone home, which gave me the chance to spend some time alone with Marcus. I felt like it had to be more to the way he was feeling, so I couldn't wait for us to be alone. My thinking during this time was that I could get his most intimate thoughts on the subject, and that maybe he was holding back some of his anger. If I could just get it out of him, this would give me the chance to explain my side of the story. With us being alone, however, this still didn't happen. He stayed firm on his belief that everything happened the way it was supposed to. Maybe he was just as overwhelmed by the moment as I was, or maybe this was just going to take some more time.

Nevertheless, we still managed to share a great conversation that night. He told me the things he wanted out of life, and with regard to these things, they were quite similar to what I still wanted. He said to me, "Meeting you was the missing piece to the puzzle." Growing up, he always felt like an alien in his own family. He could always sense that something was different when it came to the relationship between him and his family and the way they treated his sisters.

Subconsciously, the family would favor his sisters, and this would quite naturally create questions in him. He struggled to understand and would just write it off as him being the oldest. I got the sense that meeting me was the closure he needed. He could finally see why he was so different from everyone else in his household. I think that unless you really know who you are, you can never be the best *you* that you can be.

Meeting me was needed on so many levels, but I never could fully understand this in the past. I was starting to realize this whole thing was truly beyond me. Something definitely had a hand in this happening now, and it felt like its sole interest was putting our best interest at heart. It was as if it knew what was best for both of us, and it was helping us during a time where we couldn't help ourselves. During the course of the conversation, something really profound happened that sent me in a direction of serving great purpose in my life. While sitting there staring at my son, I had the most intelligent and clear thought I've ever had thus far. This thought came to me and produced what we call a dawning moment. A light came on in my head, and the nature of it was so self-assuring. I knew I was on to something, and at the same time my son shared that exact same thought. We both looked at each other and simultaneously said, "DNA is so serious!"

Laughing as we shared this sentiment, I again realized this young man hadn't been around me his whole life, and yet we were so much alike. At this point, I knew it could only be genetics that produced such likeness. By no means was this learned behavior, and, throughout our conversation, I had the feeling I was sitting beside myself. As I sat pondering the thought of DNA, I suggested to my son that if they ever discovered all the secrets that lie within DNA, then they'd probably discover the truth about where we all come from, or should I say how we all were created.

It was getting late, so I decided to take my son home. When I returned home, I found myself sitting in my reclining chair. Staring out the window and looking up at the sky, I now felt for sure something was watching me move about my life, like I thought about before. My window was open, and I could feel the breeze coming through. It felt so calming, and I was at peace with the way things had developed. I thought about everything that took place, and was piecing it all together in my mind—the way I felt prior to meeting him, the truth that I was suppressing over the years, and the conversation we had about DNA. Then suddenly something came over me.

Oh my God, it became so clear! There could only be one who could've possibly known everything I'd been fearful of and thinking about when it came to this reunion. Who could've known that deep down inside, I really wanted to do the right thing but needed help to overcome my fears? Yes, it could only be one, and in that instance, the understanding would dawn on me, giving me the feeling like I was Albert Einstein discovering the theory of relativity. As this all dawned on me in that moment, there was no denying who that one could be. Not only did I feel his presence, but I felt as if I could see him! When I say I could see him, it's all about the understanding. I didn't physically lay my eyes on him, but with my vision, he was certainly there. What made it all come together was the timing, leaving me to realize everything has a purpose. If not for the way things happened in my life, there was no way I could've come to this conclusion. I couldn't believe what I was realizing, and this moment in time was one I would never forget as long as I remain on this earth. Looking out my window and staring at the sky, I could see plain as day that this was all planned out. Everything that happened with me and my son happened for a reason.

Over the years, we had several opportunities where our paths could have crossed, but they hadn't. If they had, the same feelings and realization wouldn't have occurred. I was in a particular place in my life due to the events that had recently taken place. If it was any other time, I couldn't say what dawned on me now, would've dawned on me then. Understanding this was strategically done, and, having that morning light in my head, my vision became ever so bright. I could see clearly that there could only be one who would know all that I was thinking and all that I was fearful of with regard to my son. I also realized that as much as I tried to prevent this from happening, I really didn't have any control over the events whatsoever. I realized that the three recent events in my life were related. Each event was conditioning me for the next one to come. If not for the previous event, I would've never been able to process what was happening in the way that I did. Donnal was such a sweet guy, and in my heart I felt he didn't deserved to die because my thoughts on death was that it is the end for us; nothing left but eternal darkness. To see and feel his presence and have the spirit of him still being demonstrated in my life through his family, gave me the greatest feeling of hope to combat that great feeling of fear I had about death. I had never experienced such peace before in my life, but that was just the tip of the iceberg.

Now, my mind was ready for what was coming. To have one of my best friends, Ronald, taken away without giving me a chance to reconcile left another feeling in me. This feeling was emptiness, a sense of emptiness I've never felt before. Right when the example of Donnal's life began influencing me to look within my heart and share what's there, I was ready to reach out to Ronald yet again only to have that not be available to me. No, this feeling would be much diffcrent from the one before, but it was very necessary in order for me to seek out. I couldn't understand why that great feeling had to be taken away. Just one week after Donnal's passing, the news of Ron passing left me at an all-time low, and, now in my own way, I would begin to look for answers, answers that I didn't even know.

Last but not the least, here comes my son. Every time we feel like life has nothing left to give us, out of nowhcre comes a great surprise. In my case, it was two great surprises. Never in a million years would I had been able to see this coming, not even after my friend, Keith, forewarned me. All the things that were happening were leading up to me gaining the fulfillment that would last me a lifetime. That fulfillment centered on the idea that there was nothing for me to be afraid of and took me back to that feeling of peace. What was waiting for me around the corner of life was my son, the only person who could lead me to understanding that the greatest relationship I have has been there for me all along.

Now, the question became the answer for me, and it hit me like a flash of lightning—who else could it be but God? Who else has the ability to probe the mind and know what you're thinking and feeling and has the capability to reveal these things to you? And not only reveal these things but also relieve you of the stress caused by the worrying, which had plagued your mind for years, while your answer was to pretend the circumstances didn't exist. Who else could it be? As I gave it a thought, what followed instantaneously was the answer. The answer was that it could only be one! One, who I knew and believed, has the capability to exist in all things and deliver us from our most vulnerable state, assuring us everything is going to be all right. Yes, both the question and the answer for me was, *Who else could it be but God?* In that very moment of my life, it's safe to say that

God revealed himself to me. And for me, there could be no better revelation I could have!

THE EPILOGUE

Seeing my son for the first time in twenty years taught me all I would need to know moving forward. It taught me that kids are the blessing, not the burden, and that we should never abandon our children. Besides making life easier for them, it also makes life easier for us. Through the reproduction of life, an understanding gets fostered into the conscious mind, revealing to you who resides within you and what you're capable of. What I've also discovered is that the unconditional love from my *helper* was what brought me through. It started with him, and it's the understanding of him that I will be trying to rely on in times of despair. I also believe he facilitated the reunion and prepared us both for what we would understand as a result of that day. I also understand that he used the relationships in my life to show me the ultimate relationship that's been there for me all along. And this relationship will be all I need to help build better relationships with people in the future. Relationships are our most valued resource, and some of the clichés we live by may have been influencing us to damage one of the most important things we need. With my understanding of this, please allow me to leave you with some spoken words to express my love. I entitled this "Just Knowing You're There."

Just Knowing You're There
I was once faced with a fear of rejection
That had overtaken my consciousness to the point
All I could see was a nightmare
This nightmare kept rearing its ugly head
Giving me many sleepless nights afraid to close my
eyes
For fear of the image I would see as a result of the
rejection
Somehow I would be able to clear my head
By putting aside and pretending
The inevitable would never happen
It would all go away if I just stuck to the plan
Of living my life like it never existed
This too, was your grace.
Your grace held me in this regard
Only for so long
Because you knew what was in my best interest.
What was in my best interest was to face the reality
Of what my actions caused, and this would show me
That you've always been there.
With my hands being forced in the matter
I faced my fear only to have acceptance become the
reality that was awaiting me.
But how could this be?
I couldn't see past the fear well enough,
To realize hope exists in all situations,
And with you, everything and anything is possible.
I had my heart and mind settled on the matter,

Only for it to be changed; forever; in my moment
of truth.
My moment of truth was the sweetest joy,
Because as a result of the acceptance I gained a new
life and a greater understanding,
That all my fears could be cast away by the simple
fact that you've always been there.
"Just knowing you're there"
Gave me the feeling of what true love really feels
like.
"Just knowing you're there"
Made the world become a different place right
before my eyes.
"Just Knowing You're there"
The pain from disappointments from the past,
Are only lessons learned for the future.
"Just knowing you're there"
Has given me the confidence,
To live my life free inside each moment.
"Just knowing you're there"
Inspires me to reach out to others,
In a way I never have before.
"Just knowing you're there"
Encourages me to build relationships with the
human race;
The race we all belong to, and need.
"Just knowing you're there"
Changes my view of life,
and I understand now, we all have purpose.
"Just knowing you're there"

Enables me to make at least one prediction
regarding my future
"Just knowing you're there"
I realize now it's not what I'm looking to see in a
woman,
But it's how she makes me feel.
"Just knowing you're there"
I never have to force the issues,
Just let the issues come to be.
"Just knowing you're there"
I can finally say I found what it is,
That all my life I've been searching for.
"Just knowing you're there"
My life is now forever complete,
And I know you'll never leave my side,
Because now I realize, that you've always been there.

My revelation that God is real was an incredible one, but I still needed more. All my life, I couldn't see past reality enough to believe whole-heartedly, so it was going to take more for me to be convinced. Without a shadow of a doubt, I could feel that what was happening was real. But I wanted confirmation. Where would I find this confirmation? Where would I go from here? These questions burned inside of me for days, and the events that took place after again inspired me to share. For now, I would just like to say thank you and ask you all to join me on my journey as I share what I discovered as a result of God revealing himself to me. Please stay tuned because there's so much more to come. The follow up story is called *Believe*. I love you all with all my heart. Godspeed.